The New Inn at Gloucester

The Story of
ELIZABETHAN
Drama

By G. B. HARRISON, M.A.

*Sometime Exhibitioner of Queens' College; Assistant
Lecturer in English Literature at King's
College, University of London; Author
of* Shakespeare's Fellows, *etc.*

OCTAGON BOOKS

A DIVISION OF FARRAR, STRAUS AND GIROUX

New York   1973

First published 1924

Reprinted 1973
by permission of Cambridge University Press

OCTAGON BOOKS
A DIVISION OF FARRAR, STRAUS & GIROUX, INC.
19 Union Square West
New York, N. Y. 10003

Library of Congress Cataloging in Publication Data

Harrison, George Bagshawe, 1894—
    The story of Elizabethan drama.

    Reprint of the 1924 ed.

    CONTENTS: Introduction: The university wits.—Thomas Kyd
and the Spanish tragedy.—Bibliography (p.   ). [etc.]
    1. English drama—Early modern and Elizabethan—History
and criticism.   I. Title.

PR651.H35   1973   822′.3′09   73-681
ISBN 0-374-93688-9

Printed in U.S.A. by
NOBLE OFFSET PRINTERS, INC.
New York, N.Y. 10003

TO
S·C·R

PREFACE

THIS small book has been written for those who have not hitherto become acquainted with the Elizabethan dramatists, in the hope that they may be tempted into one of the most fascinating fields of English literature. As it is a book for beginners, I have thought it best to omit a multiplicity of references to authorities; but, as some readers may perhaps feel inclined to read further, a short reading list has been added.

Explanatory directions have been added in many of the extracts quoted from the plays. These additions to the text may seem a little sacrilegious, but I hope to justify the method in *The New Readers' Shakespeare* which Messrs Harrap are publishing in the near future.

I should like to thank especially my friend, and former teacher, Mr S. C. Roberts, for his help and interest in this little book and at all other times. For the picture of the New Inn at Gloucester I am indebted to Mr F. L. Greenhough.

G. B. HARRISON

King's College, London
2 *October* 1924

CONTENTS

ILLUSTRATIONS

The Story of
ELIZABETHAN DRAMA

Introduction

WHEN we go to the theatre, we see a combination of several different kinds of art. Actor, producer and dramatist, each work together to produce the play; and none can do without the other. The actor's art is to portray emotion and character by spoken word and gesture, whilst the producer is responsible for giving the actor every possible aid to help him in his difficult art. But clearly the author is the most important person of the three because he provides the play itself. Great drama is thus a combination of the arts, but a very passing combination, because the complete play lives only for the moment—just so long as it takes in the performing. Once the curtain has fallen on the last act, all the elements fall apart. The actors go home; the costumes are put away; only the soul of the play remains in the author's book.

Just as all great music is composed to be heard, so all great drama is written to be acted on a stage. The theatre therefore is the proper place in which to appreciate a play. But as it is an arduous and costly business to produce a play, very often we are forced to make our own theatre, and to see many of the greatest plays acted in the imagination. Sometimes, strangely enough, this is a more satisfactory way of seeing a play because imagination is free and unbounded whilst stage-managers are tied and cramped by all sorts of restrictions; and even actors are not all worth seeing. "Heard songs are sweet, but those unheard are sweeter." If we learn to use our imagination in the right way, we shall often be able to see a play whenever we care to take down the book from our shelves; and in that great theatre which we all have in our minds, the setting, the acting and the harmony of the whole drama may be far finer than on any stage made with hands.

The highest forms of art usually have their origin in religion. Greek drama—one of the greatest of the gifts of the Ancient World—was part of the worship of the Wine God Dionysus, who was honoured in Athens by yearly competitions in Tragedy and Comedy. So, too, in our own country, Elizabethan drama, by which title we rather loosely class the plays produced between about 1580 and 1620, had its beginnings in the mediaeval Church.

In the middle ages the early 'Mystery' or 'Miracle' Plays setting forth some story from the Bible or the lives of the Saints were acted in church. Gradually, as acting became more popular, the church was often found to be too small, and so spectacles, more magnificent, were staged in market-places or open spaces. These religious plays took many forms and became very elaborate. Sometimes, as in the Coventry Mysteries, the Town Guilds each performed their own episode on a movable stage which was wheeled from place to place so that the whole drama was unfolded at different stations in the city. Sometimes a great arena was made, surrounded by a number of little stages, each representing a different locality.

But these early 'Mysteries' were very different from the Nativity Plays which many churches perform nowadays about Christmas time, for the mediaeval Christian, who lived a hard, drab life, by way of contrast, took his religion cheerfully and even boisterously. Some stories, such as the Crucifixion, were naturally acted with dignity and reverence; but others were treated with much less respect, and the characters were drawn with broad humour. The 'Shepherds Play' in the Wakefield Mysteries is pure farce.

The accession of Henry the Seventh brought many changes. Firm government and deliberate policy directed the attention of the great lords to the pursuits of peace. Two generations later, when the New Learning had taken root in England, the Reformation wrought still further revolution.

With the coming of the Renaissance, Miracle Plays began to give place to 'Moralities,' allegorical dramas in which such characters as

Fellowship, Knowledge, Beauty and the like typified certain truths. One of the best of these Moralities is the famous *Everyman*. Allegory on the whole is apt to be tedious. Even the greatest of English allegories—*Pilgrim's Progress*—owes its lasting popularity to the fact that Bunyan is more of an artist than a preacher. However, the Morality Play, although not exciting to modern taste, had a great influence on the development of the drama; particularly it created one very English figure—the Vice or Devil, who was always an exceedingly comic person and indispensable in a popular play. The comic Devil turns up in all sorts of unexpected places and it was long before dramatists could finally banish him from the stage. But the Vice has almost disappeared from England now; he survives only at street corners in the hero of the immortal drama of *Punch and Judy*.

Even reformations leave the leopard's spots unchanged. The monasteries were dissolved and ruined; the Church was transformed; but the old love of drama, being deep-rooted, survived all these movements. With the spread of classical learning, scholars and schoolmasters began to take up the Roman dramatists, especially Plautus and Seneca; undergraduates acted their Latin comedies at the Universities— Queen Elizabeth attended a performance of the *Aulularia* in King's College Chapel, Cambridge, on 6 August 1564; and schoolboys performed their annual play as part of the Christmas festivities.

Some very interesting details survive of these early amateur actors. At Oxford and Cambridge the authorities encouraged plays[1], though there was often trouble. In 1583, for instance, one Mudde was imprisoned, but released after making apology "because in a comedy which he had composed he had censured and too saucily reflected on the Mayor of Cambridge." Another offender was not so lucky; he "had made assault with a club and thrown stones when a play was exhibited in the College of Corpus Christi." For this "he was beaten with rods before all the youth of the University in the Public School Street." It is an illuminating side-light on University drama to learn that the College authorities usually had the windows removed before the play began.

Public Schools, too, had their plays and some-times they were honoured with the presence of the Queen. Thus in 1564, she went to see the "children of the grammar school in the Colledge of Westminster" act *Heautontimoroumenos* and *Miles Gloriosus*. These plays cost 59s. 9d. to stage—a large sum in those days—and the children were evidently looked after carefully, as the accounts include the following items:

Imprimis at yᵉ rehersing before Sir
   Thomas Benger for pinnes and sugar
    candee -   -   -   -   -   vi d
It. for Frankincense -   -   -   -   i d
It. for sugar candee for the children -   ii d

---

[1] They did not, however, encourage the professional companies and sometimes paid them to go away.

It. to Wm Smythe for ayall paper inke and
colores for the wryting of greate letters
and for a box of comfetts for the
children -   -   -   -   - iii s iii d
It. for butterd beere for yᵉ children being
horse -   -   -   -   -   - xii d

Most of these early amateur plays were, of
course, in Latin, but gradually as it dawned on
scholars that England had a language of her
own, they turned their hands to play-writing
and composed a few plays in English, such as
Ralph Roister Doister, but still closely modelled
on Latin patterns.

The first writer to achieve any considerable
success in this type of play was John Lyly who
produced several Court comedies, of which
perhaps the best is *Endimion*. Lyly, however,
is chiefly famous as the originator of 'euphuism,'
a term rather loosely applied to the highly
artificial and 'conceited' prose which was so
popular amongst Elizabethan writers. *Euphues*
was a deliberate attempt to show that the English
tongue, hitherto supposed to be 'vulgar,' was
capable of style, and in the novel Lyly gives an
example of what he considered fine and learned
writing. *Euphues* is exceedingly dull to modern
readers who hold that simplicity—saying a plain
thing in a plain way—is the mark of good prose.
Euphuists, however, despised such hempen
homespun. This, for instance, is how Lyly
moralises on the not uncommon theme that
young men who think themselves clever often
waste their talents and their wealth.

Too much study doth intoxicate their brains, for (say they) although iron, the more it is used the brighter it is, yet silver with much wearing doth waste to nothing: though the cammock the more it is bowed down the better it serveth, yet the bow the more it is bent and occupied, the weaker it waxeth; though the camomile the more it is trodden and pressed down, the more it spreadeth, yet the violet the oftener it is handled and touched, the sooner it withereth and decayeth. Besides this, a fine wit, a sharp sense, a quick understanding, is able to attain to more in a moment or a very little space, then a dull and blockish head in a month. The scythe cutteth far better and smoother then the saw, the wax yieldeth better and sooner to the seal then the steel to the stamp: the smooth and plain beech is easier to be carved then the knotty box.

For neither is there any thing but that hath his contraries. Such is the nature of these novices that think to have learning without labour, and treasure without travail: either not understanding or else not remembering that the finest edge is made with the blunt whetstone: and the fairest jewel fashioned with the hard hammer.

Broadly speaking, then, euphuism denotes the common Elizabethan trick of playing with words, fancies and conceits. In dramatic dialogue, it appears as follows:

[Endimion is in love with Cynthia: Tellus with Endimion.]

⟨*Enter* TELLUS.⟩

TELLUS. Yonder I espy Endimion. I will seem to suspect nothing, but soothe him, that seeing I cannot obtain the depth of his love, I may learn the height of his dissembling:...How now, Endimion, always solitary? no company but your own thoughts? no friend but melancholy fancies?

ENDIMION. You know (fair Tellus) that the sweet remembrance of your love is the only companion of my life, and thy presence my paradise: so that I am not alone when nobody is with me, and in heaven itself when thou art with me.

TELL. Then you love me, Endimion?

END. Or else I live not, Tellus.

TELL. Is it not possible for you, Endimion, to dissemble?

END. Not, Tellus, unless I could make me a woman.

TELL. Why, is dissembling joined to their sex inseparable? as heat to fire, heaviness to earth, moisture to water, thinness to air?

END. No, but found in their sex, as common as spots upon doves, moles upon faces, caterpillars upon sweet apples, cobwebs upon fair windows.

TELL. Do they all dissemble?

END. All but one.

TELL. Who is that?

END. I dare not tell. For if I should say you, then would you imagine my flattery to be extreme; if another, then would you think my love to be but indifferent.

TELL. You will be sure I shall take no vantage of your words. But in sooth, Endimion, without more ceremonies, is it not Cynthia?

END. You know, Tellus, that of the gods we are forbidden to dispute, because their deities come not within the compass of our reasons; and of Cynthia we are allowed not to talk but to wonder, because her virtues are not within the reach of our capacities.

TELL. Why, she is but a woman.

END. No more was Venus.

TELL. She is but a virgin.

END. No more was Vesta.

TELL. She shall have an end.

END. So shall the world.

TELL. Is not her beauty subject to time?

END. No more than time is to standing still.

TELL. Wilt thou make her immortal?

END. No, but incomparable.

TELL. Take heed, Endimion, lest like the wrestler, in Olympia, that striving to lift an impossible weight caught an incurable strain, thou by fixing thy thoughts above thy reach, fall into a disease without all recure. But I see thou art now in love with Cynthia.

END. No, Tellus; thou knowest that the stately cedar, whose top reacheth unto the clouds, never boweth his head to the shrubs that grow in the valley; nor ivy, that climbeth up by the elm, can ever get hold of the beams of the sun; Cynthia[1] I honour in all humility, whom none ought, or dare adventure to love; whose affections are immortal, and virtues infinite. Suffer me therefore to gaze on the Moon, at whom, were it not for thyself, I would die with wondering.

This type of play was never popular with the mass of the people who still enjoyed the old Mysteries and Moralities. For some time there was a sharp distinction between 'classical' and 'homegrown' drama. The courtier and the scholar shared the contempt for 'naughty playmakers' which Sir Philip Sidney had expressed in the *Apologie for Poetrie* (*c.* 1580).

Sidney unfortunately died before the professional stages had produced any dramas of note and so his censures are not of very great value; had he seen the products of the next

---

[1] By Cynthia, the Moon Goddess (= Diana, the Virgin Huntress), is implied Elizabeth the Virgin Queen. Compare Shakespeare's flattery of the "fair vestal, throned by the west" (*Midsummer-Night's Dream*, II. i. 158).

generation, he would doubtless have changed his mind. His main objection was that playwriters did not keep to the 'rules' which had been evolved from the observations of the Greek philosopher Aristotle in his *Poetics*. Now as Aristotle had only known a highly conventional form of religious drama, his remarks were naturally only applicable to the peculiar conditions of the Greek stage. The auditorium was enormous—at Athens it is said to have held 30,000 spectators; and the stage was long and narrow so that the effect, from the point of view of the audience, was that of a bas-relief. Moreover, in order to be seen by so vast an assembly, the actors wore high masks, stately robes and enormous boots, called buskins, which much hindered their movements. Accordingly there was little movement on the stage in the performance of a Greek Tragedy; stirring events were not shown on the stage but described by a 'messenger.'

Aristotle suggested—for his remarks in the *Poetics* are suggestions rather than rules—that Tragedy should preserve 'unity,' and by that he meant that the author should not let his plot ramble but should choose a moment in the story when a series of events happened at the same time and place. This was common sense. Aristotle's followers, however, and particularly some of the Italian critics whom Sidney admired, expanded these views and evolved what was known as the theory of 'Verisimilitude,' with the three 'Dramatic Unities,' of place, time and action. They believed—in theory—that when they went to the play the incidents shown on the stage should be imagined as really going on before their eyes. Everything therefore, such as intervals between acts, or changes of scene, which interrupted the play was to be condemned. Hence the story had to be so arranged that all the events happened in one place and only took so long on the stage as they actually would have done in real life. Of course, this theory was seldom carried out in practice because the number of plots which can be begun and ended in three hours, or even twenty-four for that matter, is very limited.

However, Sidney and the rest of the learned literary men believed these rules, and accordingly they regarded the professional writers, whose work so far was indeed very feeble, as too vulgar for anything but ridicule. Sidney even went so far as to hold up for praise, though with some reservations, a most tedious, long-winded play called *Gorboduc* because it preserved the 'rules.'

Apart from the imported Classical drama which was an affair of scholars and men of leisure, popular dramas had been performed by two classes of actors; the Guild players in the towns, and the servants of the great lords in the great houses. These latter were really the founders of the acting profession.

One of the results of the Renaissance was a new-born love of magnificence and display. The old-fashioned Barons, who perished in the Wars

of the Roses, were half farmers, half petty kings,
and had supported hosts of retainers. The new
nobility found it impossible to pay for innumerable hangers-on and at the same time to spend
their money on personal luxury and magnificent
clothes. Hence, for the sake of economy, many
of the useless retainers were turned off. Amongst
the followers of the old nobility were those whose
duty it was to entertain the household in various
ways. In the new conditions they had to shift
for themselves, and so naturally those who had
any talent became professional players.

At first these players moved from place
to place and acted in the Inn Yards; a typical
example of these is still to be seen at the New
Inn, Gloucester, which forms the frontispiece to
this book. But in 1576, James Burbage, chief
player to the great Earl of Leicester, built the
first English theatre in Shoreditch, just outside
the walls of the City of London.

The THEATRE was built on the model of the
Inn Yard. It differed very considerably from
a modern theatre, especially in two particulars.
There was no curtain; which meant that everything had to be done in full view of the audience;
and the 'apron-stage,' as it is called, stretched
out well into the pit so that the actors were
visible on all sides. The actors were thus right
in the midst of their audience. Accordingly
Elizabethan drama was confined by certain very
special restrictions, which, incidentally, were
largely responsible for its progress. The absence
of scenery and the very close contact with the

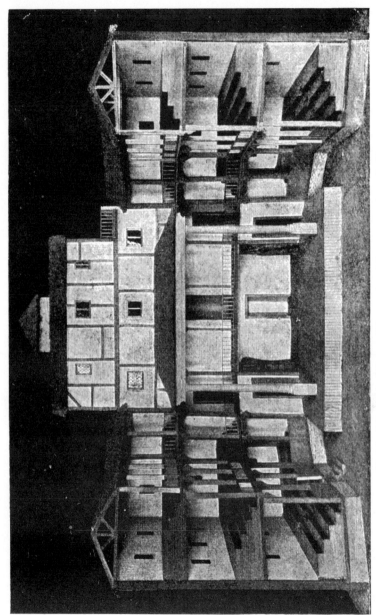

Model of the Globe Theatre (The curtains of the recess are drawn back)

spectators meant that the actor had to rely far more on his own powers of creating the illusion. Moreover, the producer's work being practically eliminated, author and actor had more work thrown on them.

The details of the stage arrangements may best be realised from the adjoining photograph of a model of the Globe Theatre.

On either side at the back of the stage were two doors by which actors entered and left the stage. In the centre was a curtained recess which served as a 'green-room' but could be used as a small inner scene by drawing the curtain aside. Over the whole ran a gallery which was used whenever the action went on 'above,' as the stage directions sometimes put it[1].

In short, the Elizabethan playhouse was a simple affair; but it is a mistake to think that it was 'crude.' Though its conventions differed very materially from those of the modern theatre, plays were staged at great cost. The actors were magnificently costumed and properties, which after all can take the place of scenery, were extensively used.

THE UNIVERSITY WITS

For such a stage, Elizabethan drama was written. Lyly was a University man and a courtier, and his plays were intended for private performance before a small, select audience; but there were others who could turn

[1] For a description of the Elizabethan stage, etc., see *Shakespeare The Man and his Stage*, chap. 3.

out just as good a play. Accordingly, from about 1585 to 1595, the play-writing business was taken over by a group of well-educated writers, known as the 'University Wits.' In their hands drama ceased to be doggerel and became literature.

First of these in time was Thomas Kyd, the son of a scrivener; though not a University man, he was certainly one of the set. He was followed by George Peele and Thomas Lodge, both Oxford men; and from Cambridge, by Christopher Marlowe, Robert Greene and Thomas Nashe. Lodge, Greene and Nashe had already made their names as novelists but were attracted by the increasing profits of dramatic writing.

It is not surprising that the University Wits should have monopolised drama. They were practised writers who knew how to please their public, and, in addition, they had been accustomed to drama from their school days. For some years after the building of the THEATRE, plays on the public stages had improved slowly. The new group scored their first success with Kyd's *Spanish Tragedy.*

Thomas Kyd and the
Spanish Tragedy

THE *SPANISH TRAGEDY* was first staged in 1585 or 1586, and was so popular that it continued to reappear for over half a century. Its author, Thomas Kyd, was an insignificant person who made a very precarious living by doing hackwork for various publishers. He had picked up a fair knowledge of the Classics at the Merchant Taylors' School under the great headmaster Richard Mulcaster and he had some acquaintance with Italian and French.

Kyd's imagination seems to have run in gory channels. In addition to the *Spanish Tragedy*, he is sometimes credited with having written *Arden of Feversham*, a murder play, and most of *Titus Andronicus*. His great speciality was plot construction, and his method was to build up a story by various dramatic devices and delays until it reached a telling crisis in the last Act.

The end of the *Spanish Tragedy* will illustrate his skill in devising 'situations.'

Very briefly the story of the plot is as follows. The Spanish armies having defeated the forces of Portugal, there meet at the court of Spain, Balthazar, the captive son of the Viceroy of Portugal; Lorenzo and his sister Belimperia,

the children of the Duke of Castile; Horatio
and his father Hieronimo, the 'chief marshal'
of the Spanish king. Belimperia loves Horatio,
but her brother Lorenzo, who is a typically
unscrupulous 'machiavellian,' had decided that
she ought to marry the Prince Balthazar.

At midnight, Horatio and Belimperia meet
secretly in the garden, but Lorenzo has spies
who tell him everything. Lorenzo and Balthazar break in on the lovers. They stab
Horatio and leave his body hanging in the
arbour. The noise arouses old Hieronimo, who
comes out of his bedroom to see what has
happened.

What outcries pluck me from my naked bed,
And chill my throbbing heart with trembling fear,
Which never danger yet could daunt before?
Who calls Hieronimo? speak, here I am.
I did not slumber; therefore 'twas no dream.
No, no, it was some woman cried for help;
And here within this garden did she cry;
And in this garden must I rescue her.—
    ⟨*He looks round and sees a body hanging in the trees.*⟩
But stay, what murderous spectacle is this?
A man hanged up, and all the murderers gone!
And in my bower, to lay the guilt on me!
This place was made for pleasure, not for death.
      ⟨*Still ignorant, he cuts the body down.*⟩
Those garments that he wears I oft have seen—
Alas, it is Horatio, my sweet son!
O no, but he that whilom was my son!
O, was it thou that call'dst me from my bed?
O speak, if any spark of life remain:
I am thy father; who hath slain my son?
What savage monster, not of human kind,

THE

SPANISH TRAGE-

die, Containing the lamentable
end of *Don Horatio*, and *Bel-imperia*:
with the pittifull death of
olde *Hieronimo*.

Newly corrected and amended of such grosse faults as
passed in the first impression.

AT LONDON
Printed by *Edward Allde*, for
Edward White.

Title page of the earliest extant edition of the *Spanish Tragedy*

Hath here been glutted with thy harmless blood,
And left thy bloody corpse dishonour'd here,
For me, amidst these dark and deathful shades,
To drown thee with an ocean of my tears?

Lorenzo, meanwhile, has caused his sister to
be shut up. Hieronimo now lives only for
vengeance; but for a long time he cannot find
out who has committed the murder. However,
ultimately he learns that Lorenzo and Balthazar
are his enemies.

Peace is made between Spain and Portugal,
and Belimperia, against her will, is betrothed
to Balthazar. In honour of the event, Hieronimo
is asked to stage-manage a tragedy. The actors
are himself, Balthazar, Lorenzo and Belimperia.
Hieronimo explains the plot to them.

           The chronicles of Spain
Record this written of a knight of Rhodes:
He was betroth'd and wedded at the length,
To one Perseda, an Italian dame,
Whose beauty ravish'd all that her beheld,
Especially the soul of Soliman,
Who at the marriage was the chiefest guest.
By sundry means sought Soliman to win
Perseda's love, and could not gain the same.
Then 'gan he break his passions to a friend,
One of his bashaws, whom he held full dear;
Her had this bashaw long solicited,
And saw she was not otherwise to be won,
But by her husband's death, this knight of Rhodes,
Whom presently by treachery he slew.
She, stirr'd with an exceeding hate therefore,
As cause of this slew Soliman,
And, to escape the bashaw's tyranny,
Did stab herself:—and this the tragedy.

LORENZO. O excellent!

BELIMPERIA. But say, Hieronimo, what then became
Of him that was the bashaw?

HIERONIMO. Marry, thus:
Mov'd with remorse of his misdeeds,
Ran to a mountain-top, and hung himself.

BALTHAZAR. But which of us is to perform that part?

HIER. ⟨*with grim irony*⟩. O, that will I, my lords; make
no doubt of it:
I'll play the murderer, I warrant you;
For I already have conceited[1] that.

The time comes for the play to be performed.
The King of Spain, the Viceroy of Portugal,
the Duke of Castile and the attending lords
appear in the gallery and take their seats.
Hieronimo locks them in. Soon after the players
enter. Balthazar as Soliman, Belimperia as Perseda, and Hieronimo as the Bashaw.

'SOLIMAN.' Bashaw, that Rhodes is ours, yields
heav'ns the honour,
And holy Mahomet, our sacred prophet!
And be thou grac'd with every excellence
That Soliman can give, or thou desire.
But thy desert in conquering Rhodes is less
Than in reserving this fair Christian nymph,
Perseda, blissful lamp of excellence,
Whose eyes compel, like powerful adamant,
The warlike heart of Soliman to wait.

THE KING ⟨*turning to the Viceroy*⟩. See, Viceroy, that
is Balthazar, your son,
That represents the Emperor Soliman:
How well he acts his amorous passion!

THE VICEROY. Ay, Belimperia hath taught him that.

CASTILE. That's because his mind runs all on
Belimperia.

---

[1] "thought that out."

'BASHAW.' What ever joy earth yields, betide your
    majesty.
'SOL.' Earth yields no joy without Perseda's love
'BASH.' Let then Perseda on your grace attend.
'SOL.' She shall not wait on me, but I on her:
Drawn by the influence of her lights, I yield.
But let my friend, the Rhodian knight, come forth,
Erasto, dearer than my life to me,
That he may see Perseda, my belov'd.

       ⟨ERASTO *enters*.⟩

THE KING. Here comes Lorenzo: look upon the plot
And tell me, brother, what part plays he?
'PERSEDA.' Ah, my Erasto, welcome to Perseda.
'ERASTO.' Thrice happy is Erasto that thou liv'st;
Rhodes' loss is nothing to Erasto's joy:
Sith his Perseda lives, his life survives.
'SOL.' Ah, bashaw, here is love between Erasto
And fair Perseda, sovereign of my soul.
'BASH.' Remove Erasto, mighty Soliman,
And then Perseda will be quickly won.
'PER.' Erasto is my friend; and while he lives,
Perseda never will remove her love.
'BASH.' Let not Erasto live to grieve great Soliman.
'SOL.' Dear is Erasto in our princely eye.
'BASH.' But if he be your rival, let him die.
'SOL.' Why, let him die!—so love commandeth me.
Yet grieve I that Erasto should so die.
'BASH.' ⟨*going up to Erasto*⟩. Erasto, Soliman saluteth
    thee,
And lets thee wit by me his highness' will,
Which is, thou shouldst be *thus* employ'd.

Hieronimo really stabs Lorenzo who falls
dead. Neither Balthazar, nor the spectators,
suspect that there is anything wrong.

    The play proceeds. Belimperia in her part of
'Perseda' stabs Balthazar in earnest and then

commits suicide. The dramatic irony is tremendous. Hieronimo has so arranged his revenge, that the fathers of Lorenzo and Balthazar actually watch their sons being murdered and unwittingly applaud the deed.

The Court clap vigorously and compliment the actors.

> THE KING. Well said!—Old marshal, this was bravely done!
> HIERONIMO ⟨*bending over the dead* 'Perseda'⟩. But Belimperia plays Perseda well!
> THE VICEROY ⟨*still ignorant*⟩. Were this in earnest, Belimperia,
> You would be better to my son than so.
> THE KING. But now what follows for Hieronimo?

Hieronimo comes forward and addresses the spectators. His strange, quiet manner makes them suspect that something has happened. He begins:

> Marry, this follows for Hieronimo.
> Here break we off our sundry languages,
> And thus conclude I in our vulgar tongue.
> Haply you think—but bootless are your thoughts—
> That this is fabulously counterfeit,
> And that we do as all tragedians do:
> To die today (for fashioning our scene)
> The death of Ajax or some Roman peer,
> And in a minute starting up again,
> Revive to please tomorrow's audience.
> No, princes; know I am Hieronimo,
> The hopeless father of a hapless son,
> Whose tongue is tun'd to tell his latest tale,
> Not to excuse gross errors in the play.
> I see your looks urge instance of these words;
> BEHOLD the reason urging me to this—

He draws forth the body of his son Horatio which has been concealed, and exposes it to the horror-struck audience.

> See here MY show, look on this spectacle,
> Here lay my hope, and here my hope hath end;
> Here lay my heart, and here my heart was slain;
> Here lay my treasure, here my treasure lost
> Here lay my bliss, and here my bliss bereft;
> But hope, heart, treasure, joy, and bliss,
> All fled, fail'd, died, yea, all decay'd with this
> From forth these wounds came breath that gave me life;
> They murder'd me that made those fatal marks....

Hieronimo goes on to tell the story of the murder of his son and how cunningly he had waited for his revenge. The Court are too horrified to move. He ends his speech thus:

> And, princes, now behold Hieronimo,
> Author and actor in this tragedy,
> Bearing his latest fortune in his fist;
> And will as resolute conclude his part,
> As any of the actors gone before.
> And, gentles, thus I end my play;
> Urge no more words: I have no more to say.

He rushes off to hang himself, but the Court now bestir themselves.

> THE KING. O hearken, Viceroy! Hold, Hieronimo!
> Brother, my nephew and thy son are slain!
> THE VICEROY. We are betray'd; my Balthazar is slain!
> Break ope the doors; run, save Hieronimo.

They come down from the gallery, break in the doors and seize Hieronimo.

Hieronimo,
Do but inform the king of these events;
Upon mine honour, thou shalt have no harm.
HIER. Viceroy, I will not trust thee with my life,
Which I this day have offer'd to my son.
Accursèd wretch!
Why stay'st thou him that was resolv'd to die?
THE KING. Speak, traitor! damnèd, bloody murd'rer,
        speak!
For now I have thee, I will make thee speak.
Why hast thou done this undeserving deed?
THE VICEROY. Why hast thou murderèd my Balthazar?
CASTILE. Why hast thou butcher'd both my children
        thus?
HIER.   O, good words!
As dear to me was my Horatio,
As yours, or yours, or yours, my lord, to you.
My guiltless son was by Lorenzo slain,
And by Lorenzo and that Balthazar
Am I at last revengèd thoroughly,
Upon whose souls may heav'ns be yet aveng'd
With greater far than these afflictions.

As they cannot make Hieronimo confess, the
King orders the tortures to be brought forth.
Hieronimo thereupon bites out his tongue and
spits it out on to the stage lest he might be forced
to betray anything against his will.

THE KING. O monstrous resolution of a wretch!
See, Viceroy, he hath bitten forth his tongue,
Rather than to reveal what we requir'd.
CASTILE ⟨*who is almost as cruel and merciless as his
        dead son Lorenzo*⟩.   Yet can he write.
THE KING. And if in this he satisfy us not,
We will devise th' extremest kind of death
That ever was invented for a wretch.

A quill pen is now brought for Hieronimo to write his confession. He makes signs that the point wants mending; a knife is sent for.

CASTILE. O, he would have a knife to mend his pen.

The knife is brought, Hieronimo makes preparations to write.

THE VICEROY. Here, and advise thee that thou write
    the troth
— Look to my brother — Save Hieronimo!

Hieronimo suddenly plunges the knife into Castile and then stabs himself before anyone can interfere.

Hieronimo, Horatio, Balthazar, Lorenzo, Belimperia and Castile are thus all left slaughtered upon the stage. Of the principals only the King of Spain and the Viceroy are left to follow the dead, as the trumpets sound a Dead March, and the mourners disappear.

Such then was the most telling scene in one of the first English plays which successfully combined the dramatic traditions of Seneca with English stage practice. From Seneca, Kyd had drawn the notion that tragedy was to be measured by the number of the corpses; but, by disregarding the 'rules,' he was able to give himself room in which to develop his elaborate but admirably constructed plot.

The *Spanish Tragedy* is the first great example of a common Elizabethan type—the 'Revenge Play.' Vengeance is one of the most primitive passions. According to Greek morality, a son was obliged to revenge the murder of his father, and many classical plays deal with this theme. In the trilogy of plays known as the *Oresteia* (the *Agamemnon*, *Choephori* and *Eumenides*) Aeschylus dealt with the terrible moral problems which arose when Clytemnaestra slew her husband Agamemnon for the wrongs he had done her. Their son Orestes was thus faced with the awful alternative of slaying his mother or committing the sin of impiety by leaving his father's murder unavenged.

Elizabethan men of letters, however, had rather a half-hearted respect for the austerities of Greek drama, but they revelled in Seneca who gave them the old stories with more blood and less morality. They heard, too, from Italy many true and terrible stories of notable revenges. So that they regarded Hieronimo's deed as perfectly natural and admirable.

The *Spanish Tragedy*, of course, has its faults; there is too much violence, and at times characters meet unnecessarily violent ends for no other apparent reason than that both Kyd and his audience liked blood, writhings and agony. The language is often extravagant and ranting, whilst the rhythm is on the whole stiff and mechanical. After a few years, dramatists realised the crudities of the play and mercilessly parodied some of the more striking passages; but after all, a piece has to be popular before it is worth parodying. It is no small tribute to Kyd's work, that twenty years later actors could still make a joke of it[1].

[1] Compare for instance the scene from *Every Man in His Humour*, quoted on page 83.

Christopher Marlowe
1564–1593

THE *SPANISH TRAGEDY* is a good example of the way in which English dramatists were learning how to manage their plots. But so far there was too much incident and too little good dialogue; drama tended to be lop-sided because writers had not learned how to manage the language. There were, indeed, plenty of long declamations, but these were more often recitations in the manner of epic poetry than appropriate dramatic speeches. From quite early times plays were written in verse—one of the many differences between the modern and the Elizabethan practice. If a modern play is written in verse, there are always a number of critics who will at once cry out, "O, but people don't talk like this in real life, why should they on the stage?" The truth is that many producers still hold to what is known as the 'Theory of Verisimilitude'; everything, costume, scenery, lighting and dialogue is constructed to make us believe that we are actually seeing 'real life.' In the Elizabethan playhouse, it was obviously impossible to follow the 'real life theory.' Accordingly the dramatist and his audience entered into the spirit of the thing and used their imaginations. Indeed, in the chorus to *Henry the Fifth*, Shakespeare makes a very special appeal to the spectators to forget the limitations of the stage:

> And let us, ciphers to this great accompt,
> On your imaginary forces work.
> Suppose within the girdle of these walls
> Are now confin'd two mighty monarchies,
> Whose high upreared and abutting fronts
> The perilous narrow ocean parts asunder:
> Piece out our imperfections with your thoughts;
> Into a thousand parts divide one man,
> And make imaginary puissance;
> Think, when we talk of horses, that you see them
> Printing their proud hoofs i' the receiving earth;
> For 'tis your thoughts that now must deck our kings,
> Carry them here and there, jumping o'er times,
> Turning the accomplishment of many years
> Into an hour-glass:......

In the absence of realistic scenery, the imagination must be stimulated by other means, and the most effective of all appeals is through fine language.

Kyd's verse, which was an advance on what had gone before, was often wooden; and the lines are occasionally so monotonously regular that one is tempted to believe that sometimes he measured off the beats on his fingers. It needed Christopher Marlowe to give life, variety and rhythm to the ten-syllable line.

Marlowe was born at Canterbury in February 1564, a few weeks before Shakespeare. He was educated for a time at King's School, Canterbury, and afterwards went up to Corpus Christi College, Cambridge[1]. About 1587, when the

---

[1] Marlowe's memory is preserved at Cambridge by a tablet in the Old Court of Corpus Christi College and the 'Marlowe Society' which acts Elizabethan plays.

Spanish Tragedy was still the highest achievement of English drama, he came down from Cambridge and joined the ranks of the professional writers—mostly University men—who were making a living by meeting the increasing demand for new plays.

Marlowe caught the secret of blank verse early. He realised, consciously or unconsciously, that a strictly regular stress very soon became monotonous, but that with variety of rhythm the blank verse line had immense possibilities. In his first play, Tamburlaine the mighty conqueror thus expresses his boundless ambitions:

> The thirst of reign and sweetness of a crown,
> That caused the eldest son of heavenly Ops
> To thrust his doting father from his chair
> And place himself in the Imperial Heaven,
> Moved me to manage arms against thy state.
> What better precedent than mighty Jove?
> Nature that framed us of four elements,
> Warring within our breast for regiment,
> Doth teach us all to have aspiring minds;
> Our souls, whose faculties can comprehend
> The wondrous architecture of the world,
> And measure every wandering planet's course,
> Still climbing after knowledge infinite,
> And always moving as the restless spheres,
> Wills us to wear ourselves and never rest,
> Until we reach the ripest fruit of all,
> That perfect bliss and sole felicity,
> The sweet fruition of an earthly crown.

Marlowe had a remarkable personality. He was one of those men, born with impossible ambitions, who early become rebels against their surroundings. Unfortunately for him, in his

[handwritten annotation: this in and of itself embodies an embrace of the Renaissance and a rejection of the medieval]

own age, political freedom was not considered desirable; and, thanks to an efficient spy system, those who attempted to raise a finger against the established constitution were speedily removed. Marlowe's revolt against his times seems to have taken the form of 'Atheism'; a violent bitterness against all forms of religion appears again and again in his plays in a ferocity of word and deed whenever priests or the professedly religious are mentioned.

In his first plays (*Tamburlaine*, Parts I and II, *Faustus* and *The Jew of Malta*) he seems intentionally to have dramatised various aspects of 'Power.' *Tamburlaine* is the story of a shepherd who becomes king of the known world by force of arms; he represents Conquering Power.

The tragical history of Doctor Faustus typifies the Power of Boundless Knowledge which was the ideal of the mediaeval scholar. Faustus is the most learned scholar of his day; he has learnt all that the University can teach him— logic, physic, law, divinity, and still he is unsatisfied. He will pluck the forbidden fruit— magic.

> Divinity, adieu.
> These Metaphysics of Magicians
> And Necromantic books are heavenly:
> Lines, circles, scenes, letters and characters:
> Ay, these are those that Faustus most desires.
> O what a world of profit and delight,
> Of power, of honour, of omnipotence
> Is promised to the studious artisan!
> All things that move between the quiet poles

Shall be at my command. Emperors and Kings
Are but obeyed in their several provinces;
Nor can they raise the wind, or rend the clouds;
But his dominion that exceeds in this,
Stretcheth as far as doth the mind of man.
A sound magician is a mighty god.

Accordingly Faustus makes a bargain with Lucifer and exchanges his soul for a period of unhindered power and enjoyment. As the play goes on, Faustus is shown enjoying his terrible possession. From time to time his conscience stirs him to repentance, but Mephistophilis is always at hand with some new temptation. By the aid of his magical powers, he had called up Helen of Troy from the dead; he falls under the spell of her beauty and she becomes the longing of his heart's desire.

Helen appears.

Was this the face that launched a thousand ships,
And burnt the topless towers of Ilium?
Sweet Helen, make me immortal with a kiss:
⟨*He kisses her.*⟩
Her lips suck forth my soul, see where it flies:
Come Helen, come, give me my soul again.
Here will I dwell, for heaven be in these lips,
And all is dross that is not Helena.
I will be Paris, and for love of thee,
Instead of Troy, shall Wittenberg be sacked,
And I will combat with weak Menelaus,
And wear thy colours on my plumèd crest:
Yea, I will wound Achilles in the heel,
And then return to Helen for a kiss.
O thou art fairer than the evening air,
Clad in the beauty of a thousand stars.
Brighter art thou than flaming Jupiter,

When he appeared to hapless Semele,
More lovely than the monarch of the sky
In wanton Arethusa's azured arms
And none but thou shalt be my paramour.

In the third play, *The Jew of Malta*, the theme is the power of wealth and hate. Barabas the Jew is an early specimen in popular literature of a type of villain which has since become common in fiction—the unscrupulous 'international financier.' As he says of himself:

We Jews can fawn like spaniels when we please;
And when we grin, we bite; yet are our looks
As innocent and harmless as a lamb's.
I learned in Florence how to kiss my hand,
Heave up my shoulders when they call me dog,
And duck as low as any bare-foot friar,
Hoping to see them starve upon a stall,
Or else be gathered for in our synagogue;
That when the offering-basin comes to me,
Even for charity, I may spit into 't[1].

About 1591 Marlowe contributed *Edward the Second* to the series of 'chronicle plays' which were so popular in the decade after the defeat of the Spanish Armada. History is always difficult material for the literary artist, because in real life events seldom present clearly definable beginnings and endings. Accordingly the 'chronicle play' is often little more than a mere series of interesting episodes which have little outward connection with each other. Marlowe, however, succeeded in turning the story

[1] Compare this passage with Shylock's speeches in Act I, Scene iii of *The Merchant of Venice*.

of Edward II into a real tragedy. He shows how the King, by his fond doting on the worthless Gaveston, destroyed the love of his Queen and the fidelity of his nobles; and then, when we feel how richly Edward has deserved anything that could happen to him, our sympathies are cleverly turned towards the miserable King whose finer qualities are only revealed in the extremity of his misfortunes.

At the end of the tragedy, Edward's death is dramatised thus:

Matrevis and Gurney, the two ruffians who are in charge of the deposed king, discuss their failure to kill him by their continued cruel treatment.

> MATREVIS. Gurney, I wonder the king dies not,
> Being in a vault up to the knees in water,
> To which the channels of the castle run,
> From whence a damp continually ariseth
> That were enough to poison any man,
> Much more a king brought up so tenderly.
> GURNEY. And so do I, Matrevis: yesternight
> I opened but the door to throw him meat
> And I was almost stifled with the savour.
> MAT. He hath a body able to endure
> More than we can inflict, and therefore now
> Let us assail his mind another while.
> GUR. Send for him out thence, and I will anger him.
> MAT. But stay, who's this?

Lightborne, the hired assassin of Mortimer, enters and presents his credentials.

> LIGHTBORNE. My Lord Protector greets you.
> GUR. What's here? I know not how to conster it—
> MAT. Gurney, it was left unpointed for the nonce,

"Edwardum occidere nolite timere,"—
That's his meaning.

LIGHT. Know you this token? I must have the king.

MAT. Ay, stay awhile, thou shalt have answer straight.
⟨*Whispering to Gurney.*⟩ This villain's sent to make
away the king.

GUR. I thought as much.

MAT. ⟨*pointing to the paper*⟩. And when the murder's
done,
See how he must be handled for his labour,—
"Pereat iste"; let him have the king—
⟨*To Lightborne.*⟩ What else? Here is the keys; this
is the lake,
Do as you are commanded by my lord.

LIGHT. I know what I must do. Get you away;
Yet be not far off: I shall need your help.
See that in the next room I have a fire;
And get me a spit; and let it be red-hot.

MAT. Very well.

GUR. Need you anything besides?

LIGHT. What else? A table and a feather bed.

GUR. That's all?

LIGHT. Ay, ay, so when I call, you bring it in.

MAT. Fear not you that.

GUR. Here's a light to go into the dungeon.

LIGHT. So now must I about this gear; ne'er was
there any
So finely handled as this king shall be.
⟨*Looking round at the loathsome dungeon.*⟩
Foh! here's a place indeed with all my heart!

However foolishly Edward had behaved, we
feel that he never deserved all this. At any rate
he was a king and the sufferings which these
low-born ruffians inflict on him are greater than
any mortal man deserves.

As Lightborne enters the dungeon, the King
stirs uneasily.

EDWARD. Who's there? .What light is that, wherefore com'st thou?

LIGHT. To comfort you and bring you joyful news.

EDW. Small comfort finds poor Edward in thy looks,
Villain! I know thou com'st to murder me.

LIGHT. ⟨*ironically*⟩. To murder you, my most
gracious lord?
Far is it from my heart to do you harm.
The Queen sent me—to see how you were used;
For she relents at this your misery.
And what eyes can refrain from shedding tears
To see a king in this most piteous state?

EDW. Weepest thou already: list a while to me,
And then thy heart, were it as Gurney's is,
Or as Matrevis', hewn from the Caucasus,
Yet will it melt ere I have done my tale.
This dungeon where they keep me is the sink
Wherein the filth of all the castle falls.

LIGHT. O villains!

EDW. And there in mire and puddle have I stood
This ten days' space, and lest that I should sleep
One plays continually upon a drum.
They give me bread and water—being a King—
So that for want of sleep and sustenance
My mind's distempered, and my body's numbed;
And whether I have limbs or no, I know not.
O would my blood dropped out from every vein
As doth this water from my tattered robes.
⟨*With a return of his kingly dignity.*⟩
Tell Isabel the Queen—I looked not THUS
When for her sake I ran at tilt in France,
And there unhorsed the Duke of Cleremont.

LIGHT. ⟨*wanting to get on with the business*⟩. O speak
no more, my lord, this breaks my heart.
Lie on this bed, and rest yourself awhile.

Utter weariness overcomes the King's fears and
for a few moments he falls into an uneasy doze.
But he cannot sleep.

LIGHT. You're overwatched, my lord. Lie down
  and rest.
EDW. But that grief keeps me waking, I should sleep.
For not these ten days have these eyes' lids closed.
Now as I speak, they fall—and yet with fear
Open again. O wherefore sit'st thou here?
LIGHT. If you mistrust me, I'll be gone, my lord.
EDW. No, no, for if thou meanest to murder me,
Thou wilt return again; and therefore stay.
  ⟨*The king falls asleep; Lightborne bends over him.*⟩
LIGHT. He sleeps!
EDW. ⟨*half waking*⟩. O let me not die yet, stay, O stay
  awhile.
LIGHT. ⟨*to reassure the king*⟩. How now, my lord?
EDW. Something still buzzeth in mine ears,
And tells me, if I sleep, I never wake;
This fear is that which makes me tremble thus—
And therefore tell me wherefore art thou come?
LIGHT. ⟨*suddenly holding Edward down*⟩. To rid thee
  of thy life—Matrevis, come!
EDW. ⟨*with great weariness*⟩. I am too weak and
  feeble to resist—
Assist me, sweet God, and receive my soul—
             ⟨*Matrevis brings in the feather bed
             with which they smother the king.*⟩
LIGHT. Run for the table—
EDW. ⟨*with a great and terrible cry*⟩. O spare me or
  despatch me in a trice.
             ⟨*They lay the table on top of the feather bed and
             so hold the king down until his struggles cease.*⟩
LIGHT. So. Lay the table down and stamp on it—
But not too hard—lest that you bruise his body.
MAT. I fear me that this cry will raise the town,
And therefore let us take horse and away.
LIGHT. ⟨*the terrible business now being finished*⟩. Tell
  me, sirs, was it not bravely done?
GUR. Excellent well—Take this for thy reward—
             ⟨*He stabs Lightborne who falls dead.*⟩

Come, let us cast the body in the moat
And bear the king's to Mortimer, our Lord.
Away—

A comparison between Marlowe's *Jew of Malta* and *Edward the Second* and Shakespeare's *Merchant of Venice* and *Richard the Second* will show how much he was indebted to Marlowe. Shylock owes much to Barabas, and the Deposition scene in *Richard the Second* was modelled on the similar episode in Marlowe's play. Indeed, Shakespeare, in his early plays, was sometimes so much an imitator that scholars are not yet agreed whether many of the scenes in *Richard the Third* were written by Marlowe or by Shakespeare.

The ferocity and lack of humour which distinguish Marlowe's plays seem also to have distinguished the author. Marlowe mixed himself with revolutionary politics and would, in all probability, have ended his life at the stake or the gallows as a heretic. But whilst he was waiting to be examined by the Star Chamber, he tried to settle a private quarrel with his dagger and was fatally wounded. He was buried at Deptford on the first of June 1593.

Robert Greene
1558–1592

MEANWHILE English Comedy had been developing on the public stages. Neither Kyd nor Marlowe was likely to succeed in lighter themes; both lacked the light touch and sense of humour which are essential to a writer of comedy. Shortly after *Tamburlaine* was first staged, a new name appears amongst the professional dramatists. To his contemporaries, Robert Greene was the most famous of all popular writers, though nowadays, except to students, he is chiefly remembered for having made the first (and uncomplimentary) remark about Shakespeare. Like Marlowe he was a Cambridge man who had drifted from the University to London where he lived a wild, vicious life amongst the lowest of the people. Greene first made his name as a Euphuistic novelist and seems to have despised the stage and all who served it but, being perpetually hard up, he could not afford to let slip any chance of adding to his always insufficient income.

Greene is one of the most pathetic figures in the history of English literature. He had great talents and natural ability but his dissolute habits soon told on his constitution. He died in poverty on the 3rd September 1592 at the age of 34.

Greene's first plays were tragedies written in direct imitation of Marlowe's *Tamburlaine*. Nor did he achieve any great success until he turned to comedy.

In *The honourable history of Friar Bacon and Friar Bungay* (*c.* 1591) he introduces the famous mediaeval scientist Friar Roger Bacon and his Brazen Head. The main story, however, is the delightful idyll of the love of Lacy, Earl of Lincoln, for Margaret, a keeper's daughter. At the beginning of the play, Lacy sets out in disguise to woo the maid for Prince Edward who is not at all pleased at the thought of a political match with Eleanor of Castile. But events turn out otherwise. Lacy falls in love. Prince Edward has learnt from Friar Bacon's magic glass that he has been deceived, and is about to slay Lacy.

⟨*Enter* PRINCE EDWARD *with a drawn poniard in his hand,* LACY *and* MARGARET.⟩

PRINCE EDWARD. Lacy, thou canst not shroud thy
    trait'rous thoughts,
Nor cover, as did Cassius, all thy wiles;
For Edward hath an eye that looks as far
As Lynceus from the shore of Graecia.
Did not I sit in Oxford by the friar,
And see thee court the maid of Fresshingfield,
Sealing thy flattering fancies with a kiss?
Did not proud Bungay draw his portace[1] forth,
And joining hand in hand had married you,
If Friar Bacon had not struck him dumb,
And mounted him upon a spirit's back,
That we might chat at Oxford with the Friar?
Traitor, what answer'st? is not all this true?

---

[1] Prayer Book.

LACY. Truth all, my lord; and thus I make reply.
At Harleston Fair, there courting for your grace,
Whenas mine eye surveyed her curious shape,
And drew the beauteous glory of her looks
To dive into the centre of my heart,
Love taught me that your honour did but jest,
That Princes were in fancy but as men;
How that the lovely maid of Fresshingfield
Was fitter to be Lacy's wedded wife
Than concubine unto the Prince of Wales.

Then Margaret, going down on her knees, pleads for her lover to the still angry Prince and lays the blame on herself.

The Prince next tries to win Margaret from Lacy by the magnificence of his promises:

I tell thee, Peggy, I will have thy loves:
Edward or none shall conquer Margaret.
In frigates bottom'd with rich Sethim planks,
Topt with the lofty firs of Lebanon,
Stemm'd and incas'd with burnish'd ivory,
And over-laid with plates of Persian wealth,
Like Thetis shalt thou wanton on the waves,
And draw the dolphins to thy lovely eyes,
To dance lavoltas in the purple streams:
Sirens, with harps and silver psalteries,
Shall wait with music at thy frigate's stem,
And entertain fair Margaret with their lays.
England and England's wealth shall wait on thee;
Britain shall bend unto her Prince's love,
And do due homage to thine excellence,
If thou wilt be but Edward's Margaret.

To this Margaret replies:

Pardon, my lord; if Jove's great royalty
Sent me such presents as to Danaë;
If Phoebus, 'tirèd in Latona's webs,
Came courting from the beauty of his lodge;

THE
HONORABLE HISTORII
of frier Bacon, and frier Bongay.

As it was plaid by her Maiesties seruants.

Made by *Robert Greene* Maister of Arts.

Rob:t Green.
16 74

LONDON,
Printed for Edward White, and are to be sold at his shop, at
the little North dore of Poules, at the signe of
the Gun. 1594.

Title page of the first edition of Greene's
Friar Bacon and Friar Bungay

The dulcet tunes of frolic Mercury,
Nor all the wealth Heaven's treasury affords,
Should make me leave Lord Lacy or his love.

Such gorgeous descriptions as these are not uncommon in Elizabethan drama[1]. They express the magnificence and display, the "lust of the eyes and the pride of life" which was one of the most noticeable traits of Renaissance Europe, especially in the great Italian States. And the descriptions are not much exaggerated. But this passage is a pathetic contrast with Greene's own life "who was fain to borrow a shirt whiles his own was a-washing."

Both lovers hold out against Edward's threats and promises and in the end his better nature prevails:

Lacy, rise up. Fair Peggy, here's my hand:
The Prince of Wales hath conquered all his thoughts
And all his loves he yields unto the Earl....

The episode of Friar Bacon's Brazen Head is treated comically. Friar Bacon is discovered in his cell, lying on his bed. He has a white wand in one hand and his Book in the other. There is a lighted lamp beside him. In the midst stands the Brazen Head on a pedestal. Miles, his comic servant, stands by armed with a bill in case anything happens.

BACON. Miles, where are you?
MILES. Here, sir.
BACON. How chance you tarry so long?
MILES. Think you that the watching of the Brazen

---

[1] See, for example, *Antony and Cleopatra*, Act II, Scene ii, l. 191.

Head craves no furniture? I warrant you, sir, I have
so armed myself that if all your devils come, I will
not fear them an inch.

BACON. Miles,
Thou knowest that I have divèd into hell
And sought the darkest palaces of fiends;
That with my magic spells great Belcephon
Hath left his lodge and kneelèd at my cell;
The rafters of the earth rent from the poles
And three formed Luna hid her silver looks,
Trembling upon her concave continent,
When Bacon read upon his magic book....

The good Friar goes on for some time in this
strain until, tired out with watching and the
flow of his own words, he falls asleep.

MILES. So. I thought you would talk yourself
asleep anon; and 'tis no marvel, for Bungay on the
days, and he on the nights, have watched just these
ten and fifty days: Now this is the night, and 'tis my
task, and no more. Now, bless me. ⟨*Miles goes up to
the Brazen Head and stands admiring it.*⟩ What a
goodly head it is! and a nose!—you talk of *nos autem
glorificare*; but here's a nose that I warrant may be
called *nos(e) autem populare*—for the people of the
parish. Well, I am furnished with weapons: now
sir, I will set me down by a post and make it as good
as a watchman to wake me if I chance to slumber.
⟨*He leans up against the pedestal on which the Head
stands, and nods; then waking up with a jerk, hits his
head.*⟩ I thought, goodman Head, I would call you
out of your *memento*....Passion o' God, I have almost
broke my pate. ⟨*There is a great noise.*⟩ Up Miles,
to your task; take your brown-bill in your hand;
here's some of your master's hobgoblins abroad.

When the noise has ceased, the Head speaks
two words in a solemn voice: TIME IS.

MILES ⟨*very contemptuous of this effort*⟩. Time is.
Why Master Brazenhead, have you such a capital
nose, and answer you with syllables "Time is"?
Is this all my master's cunning...to spend seven years'
study about "Time is"? Well sir, it may be that we
shall have some better orations of it anon: well, I'll
watch you as narrowly as ever you were watched,
and I'll play with you as the nightingale with the
slow-worm; I'll set a prick against my breast. ⟨*Lest
he should go to sleep again, he leans against the point of
his bill.*⟩ Now rest there, Miles. ⟨*He nods again, and
almost runs himself through with the bill.*⟩ Lord have
mercy upon me, I have almost killed myself. ⟨*Another
great noise is heard.*⟩ Up Miles, list how they rumble.

The Brazen Head again speaks: TIME WAS.

MILES ⟨*more contemptuous than ever*⟩. Well Friar
Bacon, you have spent your seven years' study well,
that can make your head speak but two words at
once, "Time was." Yea, marry, time WAS when
my master WAS a wise man, but that WAS before he
began to make the Brazen Head. You shall lie until
you ache an your head speaks no better. Well I will
watch, and walk up and down and be a peripatetian
and a philosopher of Aristotle's stamp.—⟨*Another
great noise.*⟩ What, a fresh noise? Take thy pistols
in hand, Miles.

The Brazen Head speaks once more: TIME IS
PAST: then there is a flash of lightning, an arm
with a hammer appears and breaks the Head to
pieces.

MILES ⟨*now thoroughly alarmed*⟩. Master, master,
up! hell's broken loose...your head speaks...and
there's such a thunder and lightning that I warrant
all Oxford is up in arms.... Out of your bed and take
a brown bill in your hand...the Latter Day is come.

BACON ⟨*jumps up*⟩. Miles, I come...⟨*not realising that the Head is broken*⟩. O passing warily watched. Bacon will make thee next himself in love. When spake the Head?

MILES. When spake the head! Did you not say that he should tell strange principles of philosophy? why sir, it speaks but two words at a time.

BACON ⟨*very anxiously*⟩. Why villain hath it spoken oft?

MILES. Oft! ay marry, hath it thrice; but in all those three times it hath uttered but seven words.

BACON. As how?

MILES. Marry sir, the first time he said "Time is," as if Fabius Commentator should have pronounced a sentence...he said "Time was"; and the third time, with thunder and lightning—as in great choler—he said "Time is past."

BACON ⟨*in despair at his failure*⟩. 'Tis past indeed. Ah villain, time is past—
My life, my fame, my glory, all are past—
Bacon,
The turrets of thy hope are ruined down,
Thy seven years' study lieth in the dust:
Thy Brazen Head lies broken through a slave
That watched and would not when the head did
      will—

Miles meets a bad end. After the regrettable incident of the Brazen Head, Friar Bacon turns him out. He finds that he is no success as a scholar. At last he meets one of Bacon's devils, mounts his back, and so rides off to Hell in triumph.

Meanwhile the course of the loves of Margaret and Lacy has not run quite smooth. Lacy, not very creditably to himself, wishing to test Margaret's love, sends her a large sum of money and pretends to break off the match. But she refuses all other suitors and is about to turn nun, when Lacy arrives only just in time. The last scene of this very English comedy ends happily, as it should, with the marriages of Edward and Lacy.

Just before he died, Greene penned a letter to some of his literary friends warning them against a certain upstart crow who thinks himself "the only Shake-scene in a country." And this is the first reference in literature to William Shakespeare.

William Shakespeare

APPRENTICESHIP

APART from the Bible, no written works have attracted to themselves such a mass of literature as the plays of Shakespeare. It is no small tribute to his greatness that over one hundred thousand visitors pass through Stratford-on-Avon annually. The worship, like most other cults, is often blind; more talk of Shakespeare than read him, and his best plays are not always the most popular. Yet, when the lip-servers and cranks have been taken away, the number of those who genuinely admire and know Shakespeare's works is enormous. Occasionally the reason revolts and asks itself whether after all the work of any one man is worth all this attention, but a re-reading of a couple of the greater plays soon silences any doubt.

Where then lies Shakespeare's greatness? Mr Hales of Eton, Dryden relates, used to say "that there was no subject of which any poet ever writ, but he would produce it better done in Shakespeare." That is one answer, and it is surprisingly true. Lawyers, naturalists, sportsmen, even theologians, have in turn examined the plays and pronounced that the author must have specialised in their own particular line.

Little is known of Shakespeare's earliest work. The comedy of *Love's Labour's Lost*, written in a euphuistic strain, is probably his first complete play but, apart from this, he seems to have learnt his trade by writing additions and odd scenes for the plays of other men—much to Greene's annoyance. Such plays as the three parts of *Henry the Sixth*, although included in the list of 'Shakespeare's Works,' really contain very little of his writing. But after 1594, when both Greene and Marlowe were dead, Shakespeare emerges as the foremost dramatist of the day.

Yet even Shakespeare had to learn. As has been shown, the instrument of drama was highly developed before he began to write plays, but his earliest plays, such as *Love's Labour's Lost*, *A Midsummer-Night's Dream*, *The Merchant of Venice*, *Romeo and Juliet* and *Richard the Second*, all show similar blemishes. The touch is uncertain, the verse inclined to be rigid, and, although from the very first Shakespeare could write incomparable passages, he could also write some incredibly bad lines. The famous speech beginning "The lunatic, the lover, and the poet," ends with the dreadful couplet

> Or in the night, imagining some fear,
> How easy is a bush supposed a bear.

Nor can there be any defence when even Shakespeare is cornered by a rhyme to "destroy" and escapes with

> Speak it in French, king: say, 'pardonne moi.'

Shakespeare, in short, like any other craftsman, was hampered by his tools until he found out how to use them. But even in his apprentice days, there are scenes too high for criticism, too beautiful for any applause but silence.

In Shakespeare's playhouse, plays were acted in the open air by daylight; there was no switch for the limelight. When, therefore, the story demanded a night scene, the dramatist had to persuade the audience that they were in the dark by the force and suggestion of his poetry.

This, for instance, is how he creates moonlight on a warm Italian summer's night (*The Merchant of Venice*, Act v, Scene i):

⟨*The lovers* LORENZO *and* JESSICA *enter and whisper together.*⟩

LORENZO. The moon shines bright: in such a night
    as this,
When the sweet wind did gently kiss the trees
And they did make no noise, in such a night
Troilus methinks mounted the Trojan walls,
And sighed his soul toward the Grecian tents,
Where Cressid lay that night.
JESSICA.   In such a night
Did Thisbe fearfully o'ertrip the dew,
And saw the lion's shadow ere himself,
And ran dismayed away.
LOR.   In such a night
Stood Dido with a willow in her hand
Upon the wild sea-banks, and waft her love
To come again to Carthage.
JES.   In such a night
Medea gathered the enchant'd herbs
That did renew old Æson.
LOR.   In such a night
Did Jessica steal from the wealthy Jew,
And with an unthrift love did run from Venice
As far as Belmont.

JES.   In such a night
Did young Lorenzo swear he loved her well,
Stealing her soul with many vows of faith,
And ne'er a true one.
LOR.   In such a night
Did pretty Jessica, like a little shrew,
Slander her love, and he forgave it her.
JES. I would outnight you, did nobody come;
But hark, I hear the footing of a man.

⟨STEPHANO, *one of Portia's servants, approaches.*⟩

LOR. Who comes so fast in silence of the night?
STEPHANO. A friend.
LOR. A friend! What friend? your name, I pray you,
     friend?
STEPH. Stephano is my name; and I bring word
My mistress will before the break of day
Be here at Belmont: she doth stray about
By holy crosses, where she kneels and prays
For happy wedlock hours.
LOR.   Who comes with her?
STEPH. None but a holy hermit and her maid.
I pray you, is my master yet returned?
LOR. He is not, nor we have not heard from him.
But go we in, I pray thee, Jessica,
And ceremoniously let us prepare
Some welcome for the mistress of the house.

⟨LAUNCELOT GOBBO, *sometime servant to Shylock,*
comes calling for Lorenzo.⟩

LAUNCELOT. Sola, sola! wo ha, ho! sola, sola!
LOR. Who calls?
LAUN. Sola! did you see Master Lorenzo and Mistress
     Lorenzo? sola, sola!
LOR. Leave hollaing, man: here.
LAUN. Sola! where? where?
LOR. Here.
LAUN. Tell him there's a post come from my master,

with his horn full of good news: my master will be
here ere morning.   ⟨*He leaves them.*⟩
LOR. Sweet soul, let's in, and there expect their coming.
And yet no matter; why should we go in?
My friend Stephano, signify, I pray you,
Within the house, your mistress is at hand;
And bring your music forth into the air.

⟨*Stephano withdraws.*⟩

How sweet the moonlight sleeps upon this bank!
Here will we sit and let the sounds of music
Creep in our ears: soft stillness and the night
Become the touches of sweet harmony.
Sit, Jessica. Look how the floor of heaven
Is thick inlaid with patines of bright gold:
There's not the smallest orb which thou behold'st
But in his motion like an angel sings,
Still quiring to the young-eyed cherubins;
Such harmony is in immortal souls;
But whilst this muddy vesture of decay
Doth grossly close it in, we cannot hear it.

⟨Musicians *enter and play to the lovers.*⟩

Come, ho! and wake Diana with a hymn:
With sweetest touches pierce your mistress' ear,
And draw her home with music.
JES. I am never merry when I hear sweet music....

A few moments later Portia and Nerissa, fresh
from their triumphs over the Jew Shylock, come
upon the lovers. The moon is now down.

PORTIA. That light we see is burning in my hall.
How far that little candle throws his beams!
So shines a good deed in a naughty world.
NERISSA. When the moon shone, we did not see the
    candle.
POR. So doth the greater glory dim the less:
A substitute shines brightly as a king
Until a king be by, and then his state

Empties itself, as doth an inland brook
Into the main of waters. Music! hark!
NER. It is your music, madam, of the house.
POR. Nothing is good, I see, without respect:
Methinks it sounds much sweeter than by day.
NER. Silence bestows that virtue on it, madam.

It is a wonderful piece of suggestiveness; the subtle repetition—"in such a night...in such a night"; the underswell of sibilants; the steady presence of the stars above, "still quiring to the young-eyed cherubins"; the breath of summer night; and then as the moon sinks, the world "as dark as Erebus," and from afar one candle shining from the hall, like "a good deed in a naughty world." It is beyond the skill of human stage-managers to provide an adequate setting for such words as these.

Beside the passage of pure beauty which has just been quoted may be set, by way of contrast, a scene from *A Midsummer-Night's Dream* to show how firmly, even from the beginning, Shakespeare could handle a set of ordinary, vulgar, British working-men.

The "hard-handed men of Athens," who are rehearsing a play for the benefit of Duke Theseus and his bride, meet by appointment in a wood. The 'company' consists of Nick Bottom the Weaver, Francis Flute the Bellows-mender, Robin Starveling the Tailor, Tom Snout the Tinker, Snug the Joiner, and Peter Quince who is Stage Manager.

BOTTOM ⟨*who always takes the lead*⟩. Are we all met?
QUINCE. Pat, pat; and here's a marvellous convenient

place for our rehearsal. This green plot shall be our stage, this hawthorn-brake our tiring-house; and we will do it in action, as we will do it before the Duke.

BOT. ⟨*who has not been listening to Quince's little speech*⟩. Peter Quince—

QUIN. What say'st thou, Bully Bottom?

BOT. There are things in this comedy of Pyramus and Thisby, that will never please. First, Pyramus must draw a sword to kill himself—which the ladies cannot abide. How answer you that?

SNOUT ⟨*always full of difficulties*⟩. By'r lakin, a parlous fear.

STARV. ⟨*ditto*⟩. I believe we must leave the killing out, when all is done.

BOT. ⟨*with inspiration*⟩. Not a whit. I have a device to make all well. Write me a prologue, and let the prologue seem to say, we will do no harm with our swords; and that Pyramus is not killed indeed; and, for the more better assurance, tell them that I Pyramus am not Pyramus—but Bottom the Weaver. This will put them out of fear.

QUIN. Well, we shall have such a prologue; and it shall be written in eight and six—

BOT. No, make it two more; let it be written in eight and eight.

SNOUT ⟨*scenting another difficulty*⟩. Will not the ladies be afeard of the lion?

STARV. I fear it, I promise you.

BOT. ⟨*taking Snout's objection out of his mouth*⟩. Masters, you ought to consider with yourselves: to bring in—God shield us—a lion among ladies, is a most dreadful thing; for there is not a more fearful wild-fowl than your lion living: and we ought to look to't.

SNOUT ⟨*trying to get his word in*⟩. Therefore, another prologue must tell he is not a lion.

BOT. ⟨*pushing Snout aside*⟩. Nay—you must name

his name, and half his face must be seen through the lion's neck; and he himself must speak through, saying thus, or to the same defect,—"Ladies," or "fair Ladies—I would wish you,—or I would request you,—or I would entreat you,—not to fear, not to tremble: my life for yours. If you think I come hither as a lion, it were pity of my life: no, I am no such thing; I am a man as other men are":—and there indeed, let him name his name; and tell them plainly he is Snug the Joiner.

QUIN. Well, it shall be so; but there is two hard things; that is, to bring the moonlight into a chamber; for you know, Pyramus and Thisby meet by moonlight.

SNOUT. Doth the moon shine that night we play our play?

BOT. A calendar, a calendar! Look in the almanack; find out moonshine, find out moonshine.

QUIN. Yes, it doth shine that night.

BOT. Why, then you may leave a casement of the great chamber window, where we play, open; and the moon may shine in at the casement.

QUIN. Ay, or else one must come in with a bush of thorns and a lantern, and say he comes to disfigure, or to present, the person of moonshine. Then, there is another thing: we must have a wall in the great chamber—for Pyramus and Thisby, says the story, did talk through the chink of a wall.

SNOUT ⟨*triumphantly*⟩. You can NEVER bring in a wall. What say you, Bottom?

BOT. ⟨*loftily*⟩. Some man or other must present wall: and let him have some plaster, or some loam, or some rough-cast about him, to signify wall; and let him hold his fingers thus, and through that cranny shall Pyramus and Thisby whisper.

QUIN. If that may be, then all is well. Come, sit down, every mother's son, and rehearse your parts. Pyramus, you begin. When you have spoken your speech, enter into that brake; and so every one according to his cue.

⟨*The rehearsal begins.* PUCK *steals in behind them.*⟩

PUCK. What hempen home-spuns have we swaggering here,
So near the cradle of the Fairy Queen?
What, a play toward! I'll be an auditor;
And actor too perhaps, if I see cause.

QUIN. Speak, Pyramus. Thisby, stand forth.

BOT. "Thisby, the flowers of odious savours sweet"——

QUIN. ODOROUS, ODOROUS!

BOT.   "...odours savours sweet:
So hath thy breath, my dearest Thisby dear.
But, hark! a voice! stay thou but here a whit,
And by and by I will to thee appear."

                              ⟨*Bottom goes out.*⟩

PUCK ⟨*to himself*⟩. A stranger Pyramus than e'er played here!   ⟨*He slips out again.*⟩

FLUTE. Must I speak now?

QUIN. Ay, marry, must you: for you must understand, he goes but to see a noise that he heard, and is to come again.

FLU. ⟨*in a rapid sing-song*⟩.
"Most radiant Pyramus, most lily-white of hue,
Of colour like the red rose on triumphant briar,
Most brisky juvenal, and eke most lovely Jew,
As true as truest horse, that yet would never tire,
I'll meet thee, Pyramus, at Ninny's tomb."

QUIN. "NINUS' tomb," man. Why, you must not speak that yet; that you answer to Pyramus; you speak all your part at once, cues and all. Pyramus enter; your cue is past; it is, "never tire."

FLUTE. O,—"As true as truest horse, that yet would never tire."

Bottom stalks on; Puck has changed his head into an ass's head. He begins with great fervour

"If I were true, fair Thisby, I were only thine":

QUIN. O monstrous—O strange—we are haunted.
Pray masters—fly masters—help! ⟨*All run away.*⟩

PUCK. I'll follow you, I'll lead you about a round,
 Through bog, through brook, through bush,
  through brake, through briar:
Sometime a horse I'll be, sometime a hound,
 A hog, a headless bear, sometime a fire;
And neigh, and bark, and grunt, and roar, and burn,
Like horse, hound, hog, bear, fire, at every turn.
       ⟨*Puck dances away.*⟩

BOT. ⟨*who does not realise the change that has come over himself.*⟩ Why do they run away? this is a knavery of them, to make me afeard.

⟨SNOUT *and* QUINCE *timidly return to have another look.*⟩

SNOUT. O Bottom, thou art changed! what do I see on thee?

BOT. What do you see? you see an ass-head of your own, do you?

QUIN. Bless thee, Bottom! bless thee! thou art translated.   ⟨*Bottom is left alone.*⟩

BOT. I see their knavery: this is to make an ass of me; to fright me, if they could. But I will not stir from this place, do what they can: I will walk up and down here, and I will sing, that they shall hear that I am not afraid.

   ⟨*He begins to sing to keep his courage up.*⟩
  The ousel-cock, so black of hue,
   With orange-tawny bill,
  The throstle with his note so true,
   The wren with little quill:

All this time Titania the Fairy Queen has been lying asleep. She has been charmed and will fall in love with the first person she sees on waking. At the sound of Bottom's warbling, she wakes.

TITANIA. What angel wakes me from my flowery bed? ⟨*Titania sits up and sees Bottom.*⟩
BOTTOM *sings the next verse.*

> The finch, the sparrow and the lark,
>> The plain-song cuckoo gray,
> Whose note full many a man doth mark,
>> And dares not answer, nay;

for, indeed, who would set his wit to so foolish a bird? Who would give a bird the lie, though he cry "cuckoo" never so?
TITA. ⟨*enraptured*⟩. I pray thee, gentle mortal, sing again:
Mine ear is much enamoured of thy note,
So is mine eye enthrallèd to thy shape;
And thy fair virtue's force perforce doth move me,
On the first view, to say, to swear, I love thee.

BOT. Methinks, mistress, you should have little reason for that: and yet, to say the truth, reason and love keep little company together nowadays; the more the pity, that some honest neighbours will not make them friends. Nay, I can gleek upon occasion.

TITA. Thou art as wise as thou art beautiful.

BOT. Not so, neither; but if I had wit enough to get out of this wood, I have enough to serve mine own turn.

TITA. Out of this wood do not desire to go;
Thou shalt remain here, whether thou wilt or no.
I am a spirit of no common rate;
The summer still doth tend upon my state,
And I do love thee: therefore go with me;
I'll give thee fairies to attend on thee;
And they shall fetch the jewels from the deep
And sing, while thou on pressèd flowers dost sleep:
And I will purge thy mortal grossness so,
That thou shalt like an airy spirit go.

She calls for four fairies, Peaseblossom, Cobweb,

Moth and Mustard-seed, who enter and wait her commands.

1ST FAIRY. Ready.
2ND FAIRY.   And I.
3RD FAIRY.   And I.
4TH FAIRY.   Where shall we go?
TITA. Be kind and courteous to this gentleman;
Hop in his walks, and gambol in his eyes;
Feed him with apricocks and dewberries,
With purple grapes, green figs, and mulberries;
The honey-bags steal from the humble-bees,
And, for night tapers, crop their waxen thighs,
And light them at the fiery glow-worm's eyes,
To have my love to bed and to arise;
And pluck the wings from painted butterflies,
To fan the moonbeams from his sleeping eyes:
Nod to him, elves, and do him courtesies.

The Fairies greet Bottom:

1ST FAIRY. Hail, mortal!
2ND FAIRY.   Hail!
3RD FAIRY.   Hail!
4TH FAIRY.   Hail!
BOT. I cry your worships' mercy, heartily. I beseech your worship's name.
COBWEB. Cobweb.
BOT. I shall desire you of more acquaintance, good Master Cobweb: if I cut my finger, I shall make bold with you.—Your name, honest gentleman?
PEASEBLOSSOM. Peaseblossom.
BOT. I pray you, commend me to Mistress Squash, your mother, and to Master Peascod, your father. Good Master Peaseblossom, I shall desire you of more acquaintance too.—Your name, I beseech you, sir?
MUSTARD-SEED. Mustard-seed.
BOT. Good Master Mustard-seed, I know your patience well: that same cowardly, giant-like ox-beef hath devoured many a gentleman of your house:

I promise you, your kindred hath made my eyes
water ere now. I desire your more acquaintance,
good Master Mustard-seed.

TITA. Come, wait upon him; lead him to my bower.
  The moon, methinks, looks with a watery eye;
And when she weeps, weeps every little flower,
  Lamenting some enforcèd chastity.
  Tie up my love's tongue, bring him silently.

The Fairies take Bottom's hand and lead him
gently away.

Bully Bottom is a great man, a fine specimen
of *le phlegme Britannique*. Nothing disturbs him;
he accepts the love of the Fairy Queen and the
attentions of her sprites without the slightest
sign of embarrassment. Nor does the presence
of the great Duke Theseus and his scornful
Queen in any way upset his complacency. For
Bottom was not troubled with the gift of
imagination.

A Midsummer-Night's Dream was produced in
1595. For the next two years, Shakespeare
seems to have written little. Then, between
the autumn of 1597 and the summer of 1598,
he wrote the First and Second parts of *Henry
the Fourth* in which, for the first time, he shows
himself completely master of his craft.

Henry the Fourth, Part I is immeasurably the
greatest of all chronicle plays, though it follows
the traditional pattern pretty closely. Elizabethan plays usually have combined two stories;
the main plot deals with the adventures and
fortunes of great and noble characters; the sub-
plot is concerned with a lower order of beings

whose affairs are in amusing contrast to the historic events of the story. So, too, in *Henry the Fourth*, the history is made by the rebellion and death of Henry Hotspur at the hands of the Prince of Wales in the battle of Shrewsbury. But these heroes are dwarfed in every way by the gigantic bulk of Sir John Falstaffe, the most comic figure in all literature.

Two scenes will show the wonderful variety of this perfect play. The first takes place in the Boar's Head Tavern in Eastcheap.

In the scenes which have gone before, Falstaffe and the rest, in company with Prince Hal and Poins, had agreed to waylay certain franklins. But the Prince and Poins had devised a plot of their own. Purposely separating themselves until the robbery was completed, they had then sprung out upon their friends and so won the whole of the booty.

Poins and the Prince wait Falstaffe's return, wondering what fantastic explanation he will give of his failure.

⟨*There enter* SIR JOHN FALSTAFFE, GADSHILL, BARDOLPH, *and* PETO; FRANCIS *follows with wine*.⟩

POINS. Welcome, Jack: where hast thou been?

FAL. ⟨*looking haughtily at the Prince*⟩. A plague of all cowards, I say, and a vengeance too! marry, and amen! Give me a cup of sack, boy. Ere I lead this life long, I'll sew nether stocks and mend them and foot them too. A plague of all cowards! Give me a cup of sack, rogue. Is there no virtue extant?

⟨*He drinks.*⟩

PRINCE. Didst thou never see Titan kiss a dish of butter? pitiful-hearted Titan, that melted at the sweet tale of the sun's! if thou didst, then behold that compound.

FAL. ⟨*thumping Francis the drawer*⟩. You rogue, here's lime in this sack too: there is nothing but roguery to be found in villanous man: yet a coward is worse than a cup of sack with lime in it. A villanous coward! Go thy ways, old Jack; die when thou wilt, if manhood, good manhood, be not forgot upon the face of the earth, then am I a shotten herring. There live not three good men unhanged in England; and one of them is fat and grows old: God help the while! a bad world, I say. I would I were a weaver; I could sing psalms or any thing. A plague of all cowards, I say still.

PRINCE. How now, wool-sack! what mutter you?

FAL. ⟨*contemptuously*⟩. A king's son! If I do not beat thee out of thy kingdom with a dagger of lath, and drive all thy subjects afore thee like a flock of wild-geese, I'll never wear hair on my face more. You Prince of Wales!

PRINCE. Why, you round man, what's the matter?

FAL. Are not you a coward? answer me to that: and Poins there?

POINS. 'Zounds, ye fat paunch, an ye call me coward, by the Lord, I'll stab thee.

FAL. I call thee coward! I'll see thee damned ere I call thee coward: but I would give a thousand pound I could run as fast as thou canst. You are straight enough in the shoulders, you care not who sees your back: call you that backing of your friends? A plague upon such backing! give me them that will face me. Give me a cup of sack: I am a rogue, if I drunk to-day.

PRINCE. O villain! thy lips are scarce wiped since thou drunkest last.

FAL. All's one for that. ⟨*He drinks again.*⟩ A plague of all cowards, still say I.

PRINCE. What's the matter?

FAL. What's the matter! there be four of us here have ta'en a thousand pound this day morning.

PRINCE. Where is it, Jack? where is it?

FAL. Where is it! taken from us it is: a hundred upon poor four of us.

PRINCE. What, a hundred, man?

FAL. I am a rogue, if I were not at half-sword with a dozen of them two hours together. I have 'scaped by miracle. I am eight times thrust through the doublet, four through the hose; my buckler cut through and through; my sword hacked like a hand-saw—ecce signum! ⟨*he draws his sword to show the dented edge*⟩. I never dealt better since I was a man: all would not do. A plague of all cowards! Let them speak: if they speak more or less than truth, they are villains and the sons of darkness.

PRINCE. Speak, sirs; how was it?

GADS. We four set upon some dozen—

FAL. Sixteen at least, my lord.

GADS. And bound them.

PETO. No, no, they were not bound.

FAL. You rogue, they were bound, every man of them; or I am a Jew else, an Ebrew Jew.

GADS. As we were sharing, some six or seven fresh men set upon us—

FAL. And unbound the rest, and then come in the other.

PRINCE. What, fought you with them all?

FAL. All! I know not what you call all; but if I fought not with fifty of them, I am a bunch of radish: if there were not two or three and fifty upon poor old Jack, then am I no two-legged creature.

PRINCE. Pray God you have not murdered some of them.

FAL. Nay, that's past praying for: I have peppered two of them; two I am sure I have paid, two rogues in buckram suits. I tell thee what, Hal, if I tell thee a lie, spit in my face, call me horse. Thou knowest my old ward ⟨*he demonstrates*⟩; here I lay, and thus I bore my point. Four rogues in buckram let drive at me—

PRINCE. What, four? thou saidst but two even now.

FAL. Four, Hal; I told thee four.

POINS. Ay, ay, he said four.

FAL. These four came all a-front, and mainly thrust at me. I made me no more ado but took all their seven points in my target, thus.

PRINCE. Seven? why, there were but four even now.

FAL. In buckram?

POINS. Ay, four, in buckram suits.

FAL. Seven, by these hilts, or I am a villain else.

PRINCE. Prithee, let him alone; we shall have more anon.

FAL. Dost thou hear me, Hal?

PRINCE. Ay, and mark thee too, Jack.

FAL. Do so, for it is worth the listening to. These nine in buckram that I told thee of—

PRINCE. So, two more already.

FAL. Their points being broken,—

POINS. Down fell their hose.

FAL. Began to give me ground: but I followed me close, came in foot and hand; and with a thought seven of the eleven I paid.

PRINCE. O monstrous! eleven buckram men grown out of two!

FAL. But, as the devil would have it, three misbegotten knaves in Kendal green came at my back and let drive at me; for it was so dark, Hal, that thou couldst not see thy hand.

PRINCE. These lies are like their father that begets them; gross as a mountain, open, palpable. Why, thou clay-brained guts, thou knotty-pated fool, thou obscene, greasy tallow-catch,—

FAL. What, art thou mad? art thou mad? is not the truth the truth?

PRINCE. Why, how couldst thou know these men in Kendal green, when it was so dark thou couldst not see thy hand? come, tell us your reason: what sayest thou to this?

POINS. Come, your reason, Jack, your reason.

FAL. What, upon compulsion? 'Zounds, an I were at the strappado, or all the racks in the world, I would not tell you on compulsion. Give you a reason on compulsion! if reasons were as plentiful as black-berries, I would give no man a reason upon com-pulsion, I.

PRINCE. I' ll be no longer guilty of this sin; this sanguine coward, this bed-presser, this horseback-breaker, this huge hill of flesh,—

FAL. 'Sblood, you starveling, you elf-skin, you dried neat's tongue, you stockfish! O for breath to utter what is like thee! you tailor's-yard, you sheath, you bow-case, you vile standing-tuck,—

PRINCE. Well, breathe awhile, and then to it again: and when thou hast tired thyself in base com-parisons, hear me speak but this.

POINS. Mark, Jack.

PRINCE. We two saw you four set on four and bound them, and were masters of their wealth. Mark now, how a plain tale shall put you down. Then did we two set on you four; and, with a word, out-faced you from your prize, and have it; yea, and can show it you here in the house: and, Falstaffe, you carried your guts away as nimbly, with as quick dexterity, and roared for mercy and still run and roared, as ever I heard bull-calf. What a slave art thou, to hack thy sword as thou hast done, and then say it was in fight! What trick, what device, what starting-hole, canst thou now find out to hide thee from this open and apparent shame?

POINS. Come, let's hear, Jack; what trick hast thou now?

FAL. ⟨*not in the least put out*⟩. By the Lord, I knew

ye as well as he that made ye. Why, hear you, my masters: was it for me to kill the heir-apparent? should I turn upon the true prince? why, thou knowest I am as valiant as Hercules: but beware instinct; the lion will not touch the true prince. Instinct is a great matter; I was now a coward on instinct. I shall think the better of myself and thee during my life; I for a valiant lion, and thou for a true prince. But, by the Lord, lads, I am glad you have the money. Hostess, clap to the doors: watch to-night, pray to-morrow. Gallants, lads, boys, hearts of gold, all the titles of good fellowship come to you! What, shall we be merry? shall we have a play extempore?

PRINCE. Content; and the argument shall be thy running away.

FAL. Ah, no more of that, Hal, an thou lovest me!

News from the court interrupts their play. Falstaffe goes out to see what has happened and returns to say that Owen Glendower and the Percies are in rebellion: "Art thou not horribly afraid," he says to the Prince, "doth not thy blood thrill at it?"

PRINCE. Not a whit, i' faith; I lack some of thy instinct.

FAL. Well, thou wilt be horribly chid to-morrow when thou comest to thy father: if thou love me, practise an answer.

PRINCE. Do thou stand for my father, and examine me upon the particulars of my life.

FAL. Shall I? content: this chair shall be my state, this dagger my sceptre, and this cushion my crown.

PRINCE. Thy state is taken for a joined-stool, thy golden sceptre for a leaden dagger, and thy precious rich crown for a pitiful bald crown!

FAL. Well, an the fire of grace be not quite out of thee, now shalt thou be moved. Give me a cup of sack to make my eyes look red, that it may be thought I have wept; for I must speak in passion, and I will do it in King Cambyses' vein.

PRINCE. Well, here is my leg.

FAL. And here is my speech. Stand aside, nobility.

Falstaffe, with a cushion on his head and a dagger in his hand, poses as the King.

HOST. O Jesu, this is excellent sport, i' faith!

FAL. *⟨breaking into verse of the 'Tamburlaine' type⟩.* Weep not, sweet queen; for trickling tears are vain.

HOST. O, the father, how he holds his countenance!

FAL. For God's sake, lords, convey my tristful queen;

For tears do stop the flood-gates of her eyes.

HOST. O Jesu, he doth it as like one of these harlotry players as ever I see!

FAL. Peace, good pint-pot; peace, good tickle-brain. Harry, I do not only marvel where thou spendest thy time, but also how thou art accompanied: for though the camomile, the more it is trodden on the faster it grows, yet youth, the more it is wasted the sooner it wears. That thou art my son, I have partly thy mother's word, partly my own opinion, but chiefly a villanous trick of thine eye and a foolish hanging of thy nether lip, that doth warrant me. If then thou be son to me, here lies the point; why, being son to me, art thou so pointed at? Shall the blessed sun of heaven prove a micher and eat black-berries? a question not to be asked. Shall the son of England prove a thief and take purses? a question to be asked. There is a thing, Harry, which thou hast often heard of and it is known to many in our land by the name of pitch: this pitch, as ancient writers do report, doth defile; so doth the company thou keepest: for, Harry, now I do not speak to thee in drink but in tears, not in pleasure but in passion, not in words only, but in woes also: and yet there is a virtuous man whom I have often noted in thy company, but I know not his name.

PRINCE. What manner of man, an it like your majesty?

FAL. A goodly portly man, i' faith, and a corpulent; of a cheerful look, a pleasing eye and a most noble carriage; and, as I think, his age some fifty, or, by'r lady, inclining to three score; and now I remember me, his name is Falstaffe; if that man should be lewdly given, he deceiveth me; for, Harry, I see virtue in his looks. If then the tree may be known by the fruit, as the fruit by the tree, then, peremptorily I speak it, there is virtue in that Falstaffe: him keep with, the rest banish. And tell me now, thou naughty varlet, tell me, where hast thou been this month?

PRINCE. Dost thou speak like a king? Do thou stand for me, and I'll play my father.

FAL. Depose me? if thou dost it half so gravely, so majestically, both in word and matter, hang me up by the heels for a rabbit-sucker or a poulter's hare.

PRINCE. Well, here I am set.

FAL. And here I stand: judge, my masters.

PRINCE. Now, Harry, whence come you?

FAL. My noble lord, from Eastcheap.

PRINCE. The complaints I hear of thee are grievous.

FAL. 'Sblood, my lord, they are false: nay, I'll tickle ye for a young prince, i' faith.

PRINCE. Swearest thou, ungracious boy? henceforth ne'er look on me. Thou art violently carried away from grace: there is a devil haunts thee in the likeness of an old fat man; a tun of man is thy companion. Why dost thou converse with that trunk of humours, that bolting-hutch of beastliness, that swollen parcel of dropsies, that huge bombard of sack, that stuffed cloak-bag of guts, that roasted Manningtree ox with the pudding in his belly, that reverend vice, that grey iniquity, that father ruffian, that vanity in years? Wherein is he good, but to taste sack and drink it? wherein neat and cleanly, but to carve a capon and eat it? wherein cunning, but in craft? wherein crafty, but in villany? wherein villanous, but in all things? wherein worthy, but in nothing?

FAL. I would your grace would take me with you: whom means your grace?

PRINCE. That villanous abominable misleader of youth, Falstaffe, that old white-bearded Satan.

FAL. My lord, the man I know.

PRINCE. I know thou dost.

FAL. But to say I know more harm in him than in myself, were to say more than I know. That he is old, the more the pity, his white hairs do witness it; but that he is, saving your reverence, a whoremaster, that I utterly deny. If sack and sugar be a fault, God help the wicked! if to be old and merry be a sin, then many an old host that I know is damned: if to be fat be to be hated, then Pharaoh's lean kine are to be loved. No, my good lord; banish Peto, banish Bardolph, banish Poins: but for sweet Jack Falstaffe, kind Jack Falstaffe, true Jack Falstaffe, valiant Jack Falstaffe, and therefore more valiant, being, as he is, old Jack Falstaffe, banish not him thy Harry's company, banish not him thy Harry's company: banish plump Jack, and banish all the world.

PRINCE. I do, I will.

A knocking is heard. The Hostess, Francis and Bardolph run to see what is the matter. Bardolph returns in great agitation.

BARD. O, my lord, my lord! the sheriff with a most monstrous watch is at the door.

FAL. Out, ye rogue! Play out the play: I have much to say in the behalf of that Falstaffe.

⟨*Re-enter the* Hostess.⟩

HOST. O Jesu, my lord, my lord!

PRINCE. Heigh, heigh! the devil rides upon a
fiddlestick: what's the matter?

HOST. The sheriff and all the watch are at the
door: they are come to search the house. Shall I let
them in?

FAL. Dost thou hear, Hal? never call a true piece
of gold a counterfeit: thou art essentially mad, without seeming so.

PRINCE. And thou a natural coward, without
instinct.

FAL. I deny your major: if you will deny the
sheriff, so; if not, let him enter: if I become not a cart
as well as another man, a plague on my bringing up!
I hope I shall as soon be strangled with a halter as
another.

PRINCE. Go, hide thee behind the arras: the rest
walk up above. Now, my masters, for a true face and
good conscience.

FAL. Both which I have had: but their date is out,
and therefore I 'll hide me.

PRINCE. Call in the sheriff.

⟨*All except the* Prince *and* Peto *go off to hide.*
The Sheriff *and the* Carrier *enter.*⟩

Now, master sheriff, what is your will with me?

SHERIFF. First, pardon me, my lord. A hue and cry
Hath follow'd certain men unto this house.

PRINCE. What men?

SHER. One of them is well known, my gracious
        lord,
A gross fat man.

CARRIER.   As fat as butter.

PRINCE. The man, I do assure you, is not here;
For I myself at this time have employ'd him.
And, sheriff, I will engage my word to thee
That I will, by to-morrow dinner-time,
Send him to answer thee, or any man,
For any thing he shall be charged withal:

And so let me entreat you leave the house.

SHER. I will, my lord. There are two gentlemen
Have in this robbery lost three hundred marks.

PRINCE. It may be so: if he have robb'd these men,
He shall be answerable; and so farewell.

SHER. Good night, my noble lord.

PRINCE. I think it is good morrow, is it not?

SHER. Indeed, my lord, I think it be two o'clock.
⟨*They retire.*⟩

PRINCE. This oily rascal is known as well as Paul's.
Go, call him forth.

Peto draws aside the curtain and discovers
Falstaffe fast asleep, snoring loudly.

PETO. Falstaffe!—Fast asleep behind the arras, and
snorting like a horse.

PRINCE. Hark, how hard he fetches breath. Search
his pockets. ⟨*He searches his pockets, and finds some
papers.*⟩ What hast thou found?

PETO. Nothing but papers, my lord.

PRINCE. Let's see what they be: read them.

PETO ⟨*reads*⟩. Item, A capon, - - 2s. 2d.
        Item, Sauce, - - 4d.
        Item, Sack, two gallons, 5s. 8d.
        Item, Anchovies and
          sack after supper, - 2s. 6d.
        Item, Bread, - - ob.

PRINCE. O monstrous! but one half-pennyworth
of bread to this intolerable deal of sack! What there
is else, keep close; we'll read it at more advantage:
there let him sleep till day. I'll to the court in the
morning. We must all to the wars, and thy place
shall be honourable. I'll procure this fat rogue a
charge of foot; and I know his death will be a march
of twelve-score. The money shall be paid back again
with advantage. Be with me betimes in the morning;
and so, good morrow, Peto.

PETO. Good morrow, good my lord

The scene passes to the conspirators. Round a table covered with maps and plans, there gather Hotspur, as his name implies, always impetuous; Worcester, his crafty uncle, who has schemed and organised the rebellion; young Mortimer who has a better claim to the throne than King Henry; and Glendower, the Welsh King, a dabbler in the black arts, a thorough believer in his own powers and a firm admirer of Hotspur.

MORTIMER. These promises are fair, the parties sure,
And our induction full of prosperous hope.
HOTSPUR. Lord Mortimer, and cousin Glendower,
Will you sit down?
And uncle Worcester: a plague upon it!
I have forgot the map.
GLENDOWER.   No, here it is,
Sit, cousin Percy; sit, good cousin Hotspur,
For by that name as oft as Lancaster
Doth speak of you, his cheek looks pale and with
A rising sigh he wisheth you in heaven.
HOT. And you in hell, as oft as he hears Owen Glendower spoke of.
GLEND. ⟨*very proud of his mysterious birth*⟩. I cannot blame him: at my nativity
The front of heaven was full of fiery shapes,
Of burning cressets; and at my birth
The frame and huge foundation of the earth
Shaked like a coward.
HOT. ⟨*contemptuously*⟩. Why, so it would have done at the same season, if your mother's cat had but kittened, though yourself had never been born.
GLEND. I say the earth did shake when I was born.
HOT. And I say the earth was not of my mind,
If you suppose as fearing you it shook.

GLEND. The heavens were all on fire, the earth
    did tremble.
    HOT. O, then the earth shook to see the heavens
    on fire,
And not in fear of your nativity,
Diseased nature oftentimes breaks forth
In strange eruptions; oft the teeming earth
Is with a kind of colic pinch'd and vex'd
By the imprisoning of unruly wind
Within her womb; which, for enlargement striving,
Shakes the old beldam earth and topples down
Steeples and moss-grown towers. At your birth
Our grandam earth, having this distemperature,
In passion shook.
    GLEND. ⟨*beginning to get angry*⟩. Cousin, of many
    men
I do not bear these crossings. Give me leave
To tell you once again that at my birth
The front of heaven was full of fiery shapes,
The goats ran from the mountains, and the herds
Were strangely clamorous to the frighted fields.
These signs have mark'd me extraordinary;
And all the courses of my life do show
I am not in the roll of common men.
Where is he living, clipp'd in with the sea
That chides the banks of England, Scotland, Wales,
Which calls me pupil, or hath read to me?
And bring him out that is but woman's son
Can trace me in the tedious ways of art
And hold me pace in deep experiments.
    HOT. I think there's no man speaks better Welsh.
I'll to dinner.
    MORT. Peace, cousin Percy; you will make him mad.
    GLEND. I can call spirits from the vasty deep.
    HOT. Why, so can I, or so can any man;
But will they come when you do call for them?
    GLEND. Why, I can teach you, cousin, to command
The devil.

HOT. And I can teach thee, coz, to shame the
devil
By telling truth: tell truth and shame the devil.
If thou have power to raise him, bring him hither,
And I 'll be sworn I have power to shame him hence.
O, while you live, tell truth and shame the devil!

MORT. Come, come, no more of this unprofitable
chat.

GLEND. Three times hath Henry Bolingbroke
made head
Against my power; thrice from the banks of Wye
And sandy-bottom'd Severn have I sent him
Bootless home and weather-beaten back.

HOT. Home without boots, and in foul weather
too!
How 'scapes he agues, in the devil's name?

GLEND. Come, here 's the map: shall we divide
our right
According to our threefold order ta'en?

MORT. The archdeacon hath divided it
Into three limits very equally:
England, from Trent and Severn hitherto,
By south and east is to my part assign'd:
All westward, Wales beyond the Severn shore,
And all the fertile land within that bound,
To Owen Glendower: and, dear coz, to you
The remnant northward, lying off from Trent.
And our indentures tripartite are drawn;
Which being sealed interchangeably,
A business that this night may execute,
To-morrow, cousin Percy, you and I
And my good Lord of Worcester will set forth
To meet your father and the Scottish power,
As is appointed us, at Shrewsbury.
My father Glendower is not ready yet,
Nor shall we need his help these fourteen days.
Within that space you may have drawn together
Your tenants, friends and neighbouring gentlemen.

GLEND. A shorter time shall send me to you, lords:
And in my conduct shall your ladies come;
From whom you now must steal and take no leave,
For there will be a world of water shed
Upon the parting of your wives and you.

HOT. ⟨*measuring the map*⟩. Methinks my moiety, north from Burton here,
In quantity equals not one of yours:
See how this river comes me cranking in,
And cuts me from the best of all my land
A huge half-moon, a monstrous cantle out.
I 'll have the current in this place damm'd up;
And here the smug and silver Trent shall run
In a new channel, fair and evenly;
It shall not wind with such a deep indent,
To rob me of so rich a bottom here.

GLEND. Not wind? it shall, it must; you see it doth.

MORT. Yea, but
Mark how he bears his course, and runs me up
With like advantage on the other side;
Gelding the opposed continent as much
As on the other side it takes from you.

WORCESTER. Yea, but a little charge will trench him here
And on this north side win this cape of land;
And then he runs straight and even.

HOT. I 'll have it so: a little charge will do it.

GLEND. I 'll not have it alter'd.

HOT.   Will not you?

GLEND. No, nor you shall not.

HOT.   Who shall say me nay?

GLEND. Why, that will I.

HOT. Let me not understand you, then; speak it in Welsh.

GLEND. I can speak English, lord, as well as you;
For I was train'd up in the English court;

Where, being but young, I framed to the harp
Many an English ditty lovely well
And gave the tongue a helpful ornament,
A virtue that was never seen in you.

HOT. Marry,
And I am glad of it with all my heart:
I had rather be a kitten and cry mew
Than one of these same metre ballad-mongers;
I had rather hear a brazen canstick turn'd,
Or a dry wheel grate on the axle-tree;
And that would set my teeth nothing on edge,
Nothing so much as mincing poetry:
'Tis like the forced gait of a shuffling nag.

GLEND. ⟨giving way before Hotspur's outburst⟩.
Come, you shall have Trent turn'd.

HOT. I do not care: I'll give thrice so much land
To any well-deserving friend;
But in the way of bargain, mark ye me,
I'll cavil on the ninth part of a hair.
Are the indentures drawn? shall we be gone?

GLEND. The moon shines fair; you may away
    by night:
I'll haste the writer and withal
Break with your wives of your departure hence:
I am afraid my daughter will run mad,
So much she doteth on her Mortimer. ⟨he goes out.⟩

MORT. Fie, cousin Percy! how you cross my
    father!

HOT. I cannot choose: sometime he angers me
With telling me of the moldwarp and the ant,
Of the dreamer Merlin and his prophecies,
And of a dragon and a finless fish,
A clip-wing'd griffin and a moulten raven,
A couching lion and a ramping cat,
And such a deal of skimble-skamble stuff
As puts me from my faith. I tell you what;
He held me last night at least nine hours
In reckoning up the several devils' names

That were his lackeys: I cried 'hum,' and 'well,
go to,'
But mark'd him not a word. O, he is as tedious
As a tired horse, a railing wife;
Worse than a smoky house: I had rather live
With cheese and garlic in a windmill, far,
Than feed on cates and have him talk to me
In any summer-house in Christendom.

    MORT. In faith, he is a worthy gentleman,
Exceedingly well read, and profited
In strange concealments, valiant as a lion
And wondrous affable and as bountiful
As mines of India. Shall I tell you, cousin?
He holds your temper in a high respect
And curbs himself even of his natural scope
When you come 'cross his humour; faith, he does:
I warrant you, that man is not alive
Might so have tempted him as you have done,
Without the taste of danger and reproof:
But do not use it oft, let me entreat you.

    WOR. In faith, my lord, you are too wilful-
blame;
And since your coming hither have done enough
To put him quite beside his patience.
You must needs learn, lord, to amend this fault:
Though sometimes it show greatness, courage,
blood,—
And that's the dearest grace it renders you,—
Yet oftentimes it doth present harsh rage,
Defect of manners, want of government,
Pride, haughtiness, opinion and disdain:
The least of which haunting a nobleman
Loseth men's hearts and leaves behind a stain
Upon the beauty of all parts besides,
Beguiling them of commendation.

    HOT. Well, I am school'd: good manners be your
speed!
Here come our wives, and let us take our leave.

Between 1598 and 1601, Shakespeare wrote several comedies including *Much Ado About Nothing*, *Twelfth Night* and *As You Like It*; all of them distinguished by a tone of light-hearted jollity and careless ease. These comedies are often termed 'Romantic' because they are based more on Romance than on real life, and it is not the least remarkable quality in Shakespeare's greatness that the characters—Rosalind and Viola for instance—are just as alive as those in the more solid plays.

In the earliest comedies (and the poems *Venus and Adonis* and *Lucrece* which were written about the same time) Shakespeare had shown a delight in word-play. The same characteristic reappears at this period in a much heightened form.

Selection is difficult, but perhaps a passage between Viola and Olivia will illustrate, as well as any, the euphuistic wit of Shakespeare's Romantic Comedy.

Viola, disguised as a man, visits Olivia for the first time to plead the Count Orsino's suit.

⟨*Enter* VIOLA, *and* Attendants.⟩

VIOLA. The honourable lady of the house, which is she?

OLIVIA. Speak to me; I shall answer for her. Your will?

VIO. Most radiant, exquisite and unmatchable beauty,—I pray you, tell me if this be the lady of the house, for I never saw her: I would be loath to cast away my speech, for besides that it is excellently well penned, I have taken great pains to con it. Good beauties, let me sustain no scorn; I am very comptible, even to the least sinister usage.

OLI. Whence came you, sir?

VIO. I can say little more than I have studied, and that question 's out of my part. Good gentle one, give me modest assurance if you be the lady of the house, that I may proceed in my speech.

OLI. Are you a comedian?

VIO. No, my profound heart: and yet, by the very fangs of malice I swear, I am not that I play. Are you the lady of the house?

OLI. If I do not usurp myself, I am.

VIO. Most certain, if you are she, you do usurp yourself; for what is yours to bestow is not yours to reserve. But this is from my commission: I will on with my speech in your praise, and then show you the heart of my message.

OLI. Come to what is important in 't: I forgive you the praise.

VIO. Alas, I took great pains to study it, and 'tis poetical.

OLI. It is the more like to be feigned: I pray you, keep it in. I heard you were saucy at my gates, and allowed your approach rather to wonder at you than to hear you. If you be not mad, be gone; if you have reason, be brief: 'tis not that time of moon with me to make one in so skipping a dialogue.

MARIA. Will you hoist sail, sir? here lies your way.

VIO. No, good swabber; I am to hull here a little longer. Some mollification for your giant, sweet lady. Tell me your mind: I am a messenger.

OLI. Sure, you have some hideous matter to deliver, when the courtesy of it is so fearful. Speak your office.

VIO. It alone concerns your ear. I bring no overture of war, no taxation of homage: I hold the olive in my hand; my words are as full of peace as matter.

OLI. Yet you began rudely. What are you? what would you?

VIO. The rudeness that hath appeared in me have I learned from my entertainment. What I am, and what I would, are as secret as maidenhead; to your ears, divinity, to any other's, profanation.

OLI. Give us the place alone: we will hear this divinity. ⟨*Exeunt Maria and Attendants.*⟩ Now, sir, what is your text?

VIO. Most sweet lady,—

OLI. A comfortable doctrine, and much may be said of it. Where lies your text?

VIO. In Orsino's bosom.

OLI. In his bosom! In what chapter of his bosom?

VIO. To answer by the method, in the first of his heart.

OLI. O, I have read it: it is heresy. Have you no more to say?

VIO. Good madam, let me see your face.

OLI. Have you any commission from your lord to negotiate with my face? You are now out of your text: but we will draw the curtain and show you the picture. Look you, sir, such a one I was this present: is't not well done? ⟨*Unveiling.*⟩

VIO. Excellently done, if God did all.

OLI. 'Tis in grain, sir; 'twill endure wind and weather.

VIO. 'Tis beauty truly blent, whose red and white Nature's own sweet and cunning hand laid on:
Lady, you are the cruell'st she alive,
If you will lead these graces to the grave
And leave the world no copy.

OLI. O, sir, I will not be so hard-hearted; I will give out divers schedules of my beauty: it shall be inventoried, and every particle and utensil labelled to my will: as, item, two lips, indifferent red; item, two grey eyes, with lids to them; item, one neck,

one chin, and so forth. Were you sent hither to
praise me?

 VIO. I see you what you are, you are too proud;
But, if you were the devil, you are fair.
My lord and master loves you: O, such love
Could be but recompensed, though you were crown'd
The nonpareil of beauty!

 OLI.   How does he love me?

 VIO. With adorations, fertile tears,
With groans that thunder love, with sighs of fire.

 OLI. Your lord does know my mind; I cannot
  love him:
Yet I suppose him virtuous, know him noble,
Of great estate, of fresh and stainless youth;
In voices well divulged, free, learn'd and valiant;
And in dimension and the shape of nature
A gracious person: but yet I cannot love him;
He might have took his answer long ago.

 VIO. If I did love you in my master's flame,
With such a suffering, such a deadly life,
In your denial I would find no sense;
I would not understand it.

 OLI.   Why, what would you?

 VIO. Make me a willow cabin at your gate,
And call upon my soul within the house;
Write loyal cantons of contemned love
And sing them loud even in the dead of night;
Halloo your name to the reverberate hills
And make the babbling gossip of the air
Cry out 'Olivia!' O, you should not rest
Between the elements of air and earth,
But you should pity me!

 OLI.   You might do much.
What is your parentage?

 VIO. Above my fortunes, yet my state is well:
I am a gentleman.

 OLI.   Get you to your lord;
I cannot love him: let him send no more;

Unless, perchance, you come to me again,
To tell me how he takes it. Fare you well:
I thank you for your pains: spend this for me.
    VIO. I am no fee'd post, lady; keep your purse:
My master, not myself, lacks recompense.
Love make his heart of flint that you shall love;
And let your fervour, like my master's, be
Placed in contempt! Farewell, fair cruelty. ⟨*Exit.*⟩

Meanwhile the Elizabethan public began to realise that another great writer had appeared in the person of Ben Jonson whose great play *Every Man in His Humour* was first produced in September 1598.

Ben Jonson

1572–1637

BEN JONSON had already tried his hand at a variety of occupations. His father had died before he was born (1572) and his mother was remarried to a bricklayer. Jonson himself was educated at Westminster School under the great antiquary, William Camden. On leaving school, he had been apprenticed to his step-father's trade; but as this was not at all to his liking, he ran away to become a soldier, and served for a time in the Lowlands in one of the English companies which were fighting for the Flemish Protestants against the Spaniards. He came home about 1592 and turned actor, without, however, making any great name for himself. Then he began to write plays. Finally he made his name by producing a new type of English Comedy.

Jonson was by far the most learned of English dramatists; and he knew it. His classical training had shown him that English Comedy made no attempt to conform to any 'rules' and very often simply relied for its effect on low jests and coarse buffoonery. Jonson felt that Comedy ought to have a moral purpose; it should make vice look ridiculous. With this object in view, he wrote a series of 'Comedies of Humours' as they are called, in which he introduces various characters typifying the most prominent failings and vices of his contemporaries.

The word 'humour' meant to the Elizabethan much what 'type' means to a modern psychologist. This meaning arose from the curious old theory that man's body and nature was composed of the four elements or 'humours' of earth, air, fire, and water. So long as the humours were accurately balanced against each other, all went well. But as soon as any one humour existed in excess, the temperament became unbalanced. The idea may best be shown in the form of a table.

Humour	Bodily counterpart	Temperament and complexion produced by excess
Earth	Black bile	Melancholic temperament
Air	Blood	Sanguine　　　,,
Fire	Bile	Choleric　　　,,
Water	Phlegm	Phlegmatic　　　,,

Hence a man with a hot temper was said to suffer from a 'cholerick humour' which showed itself in a fiery face. By degrees the word 'humour' came to be used to express any excessive characteristic or oddity. Jonson's Comedy of Humours is thus a Comedy of Types.

Jonson's comedy differs vitally from Shakespeare's, for he is intentionally trying to produce *realistic* portraits in order that he may satirise the type which each character personifies. But modern readers, who are not also students of the period, often find some difficulty in appreciating Jonson because the follies which

A

QVIP FOR AN VP-
ſtart Courtier:

Or,

A quaint diſpute betvveen Veluet breeches
and Cloth-breeches.

*Wherein is plainely ſet downe the diſorders
in all Eſtates and Trades.*

LONDON
Imprinted by Iohn Wolfe, and are to bee ſold at his
ſhop at Poules chayne. 1 5 9 2.

Title page from Robert Greene's *Quip for an Upstart Courtier*
(The figure on the left of the woodcut represents an Elizabethan fop)

he scourges have long since passed away or changed their forms.

In *Every Man in His Humour*, several different humours are shown acting and reacting on each other. It is an admirable play, probably because Jonson was more interested in his characters as people than as types.

A scene will show Jonson's skill and realistic method.

Mr Matthew, the City-bred fop, comes to call on Captain Bobadil, the professional soldier, to consult him on a point of honour.

Captain Bobadil is a soldier of fortune, rather the worse for wear. Like most of his class he lodges in a garret but lives as far as possible in public at someone else's expense. The garret is very meanly furnished, and Bobadil, not possessing a bed, sleeps on the bench.

He is just beginning to wake up after a late night. Tib, his landlady, comes in.

BOBADIL ⟨*wearing only his shirt sits up sleepily and yawns*⟩. Hostess, hostess.

TIB. What say you sir?

BOB. A cup of thy small beer, sweet hostess.

TIB. Sir, there's a gentleman below, would speak with you.

BOB. ⟨*horrified that one of his fine acquaintances should discover him at that moment*⟩. A gentleman! Ods so, I am not within.

TIB. My husband told him you were, sir.

BOB. What a plague——what meant he?

⟨*The voice of Mr Matthew comes up the stairs.*⟩ Captain Bobadil!

BOB. Who's there? ⟨*to Tib*⟩ take away the bason good hostess. Come up sir.

TIB ⟨*looking outside the door*⟩. He would desire you to come up, sir. You come into a cleanly house here.

MATTHEW ⟨*effusively*⟩. Save you, sir. Save you, Captain.

BOB. Gentle Master Matthew, is it you, sir. Please you sit down.

MAT. Thank you, good Captain, you may see, I am somewhat audacious.

BOB. Not so, sir. I was requested to supper last night, by a sort of gallants, where you were wished for, and drunk to, I assure you.

MAT. ⟨*much flattered*⟩. Vouchsafe me by whom, good Captain.

BOB. Marry by young Wellbred and others. Why, hostess, a stool here for this gentleman.

MAT. No haste, sir, 'tis very well.

BOB. Body of me! It was so late ere we parted last night, I can scarce open my eyes, yet; I was but new risen, as you came: how passes the day abroad, sir? you can tell.

MAT. Faith, some half hour to seven: now trust me ⟨*looking round*⟩ you have an exceeding fine lodging here, very neat, and private.

BOB. ⟨*not sure whether Matthew is being sarcastic or serious*⟩. Ay sir. Sit down I pray you. Master Matthew—in any case—possess no gentleman of our acquaintance with notice of my lodging.

MAT. Who? I sir? no.

BOB. Not that I need to care who know it, for the cabin is convenient, but in regard I would not be too popular and generally visited as some are.

MAT. True Captain, I conceive you.

BOB. For, do you see sir, by the heart of valour in me (except it be to some peculiar and choice spirits, to whom I am extraordinarily engaged, as yourself or so), I could not extend thus far.

MAT. O Lord sir, I resolve so.

BOB. I confess I love a cleanly and quiet privacy,

above all the tumult and roar of fortune. ⟨*He notices that Matthew is carrying a play book in his hand.*⟩ What new book ha' you there? What! "Go by Hieronimo[1]"!

MAT. Ay, did you ever see it acted? is 't not well penned?

BOB. Well penned! I would fain see all the Poets —of these times—pen such another play as that was! They 'll prate and swagger, and keep a stir of art and devices, when—as I am a gentleman—read 'hem, they are the most shallow pitiful, barren fellows that live upon the face of the earth, again.

MAT. Indeed, there are a number of fine speeches in this book! "O eyes, no eyes, but fountains fraught with tears."—There 's a conceit, "fountains fraught with tears"!—"O life, no life, but lively form of death"! Another! "O world, no world, but mass of public wrongs"! A third! "Confused and filled with murder and misdeeds"! A fourth! O the Muses! Is 't not excellent? Is 't not simply the best that ever you heard, Captain? Ha? How do you like it?

BOB. 'Tis good.

MAT. ⟨*thus encouraged begins a little piece of his own composing*⟩.
"To thee, the purest object to my sense,
The most refined essence heaven covers,
Send I these lines, wherein I do commence
The happy state of turtle-billing lovers.
    If they prove rough, unpolished, harsh and rude,
    Haste made the waste. Thus, mildly, I conclude."

BOB. Nay, proceed, proceed. Where 's this?

MAT. ⟨*simpering*⟩. This, sir? A toy of mine own, in my nonage: the infancy of my Muses! But when will you come and see my study? Good faith, I can show you some very good things I have done of late. ⟨*All this while Bobadil has been dressing; he now pulls*

---

[1] I.e. *The Spanish Tragedy.*

on his great boots. Matthew stops to admire.⟩ That boot becomes your leg passing well, Captain, methinks.

BOB. ⟨*modestly*⟩. So so, it's the fashion gentlemen now use.

MAT. ⟨*at last seeing the opening in the conversation for which he has been waiting all this time*⟩. Troth Captain, an' now you speak o' the fashion, Master Wellbred's elder brother and I are fallen out exceedingly. This other day, I happened to enter into some discourse of a hanger[1], which I assure you, both for fashion and workmanship, was most peremptory-beautiful and gentleman-like. Yet, he condemned and cried it down for the most pied and ridiculous that ever he saw.

BOB. Squire Downright? The half brother? Was it not?

MAT. Ay sir, he.

BOB. Hang him, rook, he? Why he has no more judgement than a malt horse. By Saint George, I wonder you'ld lose a thought upon such an animal; the most peremptory, absurd clown of Christendom, this day, he is holden. I protest to you, as I am a gentleman, and a soldier, I ne'er changed words with his like. By his discourse he should eat nothing but hay. He was born for the manger, pannier or pack-saddle! He has not so much as a good phrase in his belly, but all old iron and rusty proverbs! A good commodity for some smith to make hob-nails of!

MAT. Ay, and he thinks to carry it away with his manhood still, where he comes. He brags he will give me the *bastinado*, as I hear.

BOB. ⟨*pricking up at the fashionable word 'bastinado'*⟩. How? He the *bastinado*! How came he by that word, trow?

MAT. ⟨*blushing*⟩. Nay, indeed, he said 'cudgel' me; I termed it so for my more grace.

[1] Sword belt.

BOB. That may be; for I was sure, it was none of his word. But when? When said he so?

MAT. Faith, yesterday, they say; a young gallant, a friend of mine told me so.

BOB. ⟨*thundering*⟩. By the foot of Pharaoh! and it were my case now, I should send him a *cartel*[1] presently. The *bastinado*! A most proper and sufficient dependance, warranted by the great Carranza. Come hither. You SHALL cartel him. I 'll show you a trick or two, you shall kill him with, at pleasure; the first stoccata, if you will, by this air!

MAT. ⟨*without enthusiasm*⟩. Indeed, you have absolute knowledge i' the mystery, I have heard sir.

BOB. Of whom? Of whom, ha' you heard it, I beseech you?

MAT. Troth, I have heard it spoken of divers, that you have very rare, and un-in-one-breath-utterable skill sir.

BOB. ⟨*modestly*⟩. By heaven, no, not I; no skill i' the earth: some small rudiments i' the science, as to know my time, distance, or so. I have professed it more for noblemen, and gentlemen's use than mine own practice I assure you. ⟨*In his grandest manner.*⟩ Hostess! accommodate us with another bedstaff here quickly. ⟨*Tib looks blank.*⟩ LEND us another bedstaff. The woman does not understand the words of Action. ⟨*He demonstrates the correct position for rapier and dagger.*⟩ Look you, sir. Exalt not your point above this state, at any hand, and let your poniard maintain your defence, thus. ⟨*To Tib.*⟩ Give it the gentleman and leave us. So sir. Come on. ⟨*Matthew's efforts are stiff and feeble.*⟩ O twine your body more about that you may fall to a more sweet, comely, gentleman-like guard. So—indifferent. Hollow your body more sir. Thus—Now—stand fast o' your left leg—note your distance, keep your due proportion of time—⟨*In disgust.*⟩ Oh, you disorder your point, most irregularly.

[1] "I should send him a challenge at once."

MAT. ⟨*trying his poor best*⟩. How is the bearing of it now, sir?

BOB. O out of measure ill. A well-experienced hand would pass upon you at pleasure.

MAT. How mean you sir, 'pass upon me'?

BOB. ⟨*demonstrating*⟩. Why thus sir—Make a thrust at me—come in—upon the answer—control your point and make a full carrrreer—at the body. The best-practised gallants of the time name it the 'passada'; a most desperate thrust, believe it.

MAT. ⟨*thinking that he knows all about it now*⟩. Well come, sir.

BOB. Why you do not manage your weapon with any facility or grace to invite me. I have no spirit to play with you. Your dearth of judgement renders you tedious.

MAT. But one *venue*, sir.

BOB. VENUE! Fie. Most gross denomination as ever I heard. O the STOCCATA while you live sir. Note that. Come, put on your cloak and we'll go to some private place where you are acquainted, some tavern or so—and have a bit—I'll send for one of these fencers and he shall breath you, by my direction. And then I will teach you your trick. You shall kill him with it, at the first, if you please. Why, I will learn you, by the true judgement of the eye, hand and foot to control any enemy's point in the world. Should your adversary confront you with a pistol—'twere nothing, by this hand, you should, by the same rule, control his bullet, in a line—except it were hail-shot and spread. What money ha' you about you, Mr Matthew?

MAT. Faith, I ha' not past two shillings or so.

BOB. 'Tis somewhat with the least: but come. We will have a bunch of radish and salt to taste our wine; and a pipe of tobacco to close the orifice of the stomach; and then we'll call upon young Wellbred. Perhaps we shall meet the Coridon his brother there; and put him to the question. ⟨*They go out together.*⟩

A comparison between the extract from *Every Man in His Humour* which has just been quoted and a similar passage from one of Shakespeare's Romantic Comedies—for example the scene in *Twelfth Night* where Toby eggs Sir Andrew on to fight Viola—will show the difference in method between the two writers. Whilst Shakespeare delights in the incident for the fun which can be got out of it, Jonson uses it as a peg on which to display the mannerisms of his characters. However, although both Shakespeare and Jonson developed on their own lines, they were indebted to the common stock of Elizabethan dramatic devices for many of their most telling scenes.

Tricks of the Trade

WE have previously[1] noticed that dramatists were confined by the physical conditions of the playhouse. Corpses, for instance, were always a problem. In the 'picture-frame' stage the curtain comes down and the corpse walks off into the wings unseen by the audience. But as the 'apron stage' had no curtain, the dramatist had to arrange for the dead to be removed by the living. At the end of *Hamlet*, when four corpses are lying on the stage, Fortinbras and his army most conveniently appear and carry them off whilst the trumpets sound a Dead March. Again, after the murder of Caesar, Antony is left alone with the body, but a servant of Octavius arrives with a message and thus is able to lend a hand.

But apart from the structure of the stage, there were other restrictions, conventions and tricks which must now be considered.

In the First Folio of Shakespeare's Works, his plays are simply divided into Comedies, Histories and Tragedies. Polonius, telling Hamlet of the arrival of the players, is far more detailed—"The best actors in the world, either for tragedy, comedy, history, pastoral, pastoral-comical, historical-pastoral, tragical-historical, tragical-comical-historical-pastoral, scene individable or poem unlimited." The catalogue

[1] Page 12.

errs on the side of over-elaboration, but it does show the very mixed nature of the Elizabethan drama.

Critics have given all sorts of subtle definitions to the word 'tragedy,' but to Shakespeare's audience a Tragedy roughly meant a play in which the principal person (and preferably a host of others) was slain in the last Act. Comedy meant a play which ended happily—for the Hero. There could be death and misery in comedy. In *The Winter's Tale*, the kindly Antigonus is pursued and eaten by a bear, and some most heartless comments are made on his fate by the Clown who has also witnessed the wreck of the ship. "Name of mercy, when was this, boy?" asks the shepherd. "Now, now," replies the Clown, "I have not winked since I saw these sights: the men are not yet cold under water, nor the bear half dined on the gentleman: he's at it now." Histories had to include some historical incidents and great names, and preferably ended with the death of one king and the coronation of his successor, but historical consistency was a very minor matter. In Dekker's *Satiromastix* in which he attacks Jonson, the main plot is concerned with King William Rufus and Sir Walter Terrill; the comic plot contains Horace (who was Jonson disguised as the Roman poet) and a set of contemporary Elizabethan characters. Greene's *Looking Glass for London* tells the story of Jonah and the people of Nineveh, but it has an Elizabethan Clown, who disliking the idea of the

universal fast which has been proclaimed, hides
a bottle of beer and a great piece of beef in his
baggy 'slops.'

But whatever the type, nearly every play had
to include a comic element, preferably a little
music, and some sentimental passages. In fact
the Elizabethan playhouse gave a variety entertainment. The great acting companies usually
had two 'stars'—a Tragedian and a Clown—
and there was trouble with the less educated
spectators if the Clown was not given a good
part. Shakespeare had written some fine comic
parts, but even so the Clown was not always
satisfied and often did some 'gagging' on his
own, as Hamlet complains to the players: "And
let those that play your clowns speak no more
than is set down for them; for there be of them
that will themselves laugh, to set on some
quantity of barren spectators to laugh too, though
in the mean time some necessary question of the
play be then to be considered; that's villainous
and shows a most pitiful ambition in the fool
that uses it."

Accordingly Elizabethan plays usually contain at least two plots and sometimes more. In
Twelfth Night, for instance, there are four
distinct stories—the adventures of Viola, of
Sir Toby and his friends, of Sebastian, and
Malvolio. In *Lear* the stories of Lear, Edmund
and Edgar are even more distinct. Of course,
the various plots are usually skilfully woven
together, but it would be possible to separate
them and make a play of each.

There were various reasons for this practice. The stage lent itself to rapid changes of scene, and by alternating the appearances of the different sets of characters, the author broke up the action, gave variety and, too, was able to create the illusion of the passage of time. In Tragedy, as will be seen, the introduction of 'comic relief' often gives a startling contrast which makes the darkness appear blacker.

Another difficulty which faced dramatists was to give the audience those preliminary explanations which are necessary before the play begins. In our modern theatre, we buy a programme as we go in, and from it we learn who the characters are and where the scenes are supposed to be taking place; sometimes other details are added such as "An interval of six months elapses between Acts II and III." The good dramatist can often give most of the necessary explanations in the course of the first few scenes. In *Julius Caesar*, for instance, the first scene opens with the Roman crowd making holiday in honour of Caesar's return to Rome. Then come the two tribunes who rebuke the people for their heartlessness in rejoicing that Caesar is triumphing over their old friend Pompey. Soon after Caesar's procession enters; Cassius draws Brutus aside and, by the end of the second scene, we know exactly how things stand. The explanations have been made and the story has begun to move.

Shakespeare is not always so successful. In *As You Like It* Orlando comes on with old Adam and gives him a long, unreal explanation about events which both knew quite well already.

The Elizabethans never hit on the idea of the printed programme and so were obliged to find other ways of telling the audience such essential details of the story as could not conveniently be fitted into the dialogue. The commonest of these methods was the Prologue.

There are few Prologues in Shakespeare. There is one before *Romeo and Juliet*, a Chorus in *Henry the Fifth* which explains how the action is progressing between the Acts, and one or two others. But with most dramatists introductory prologues are the rule rather than the exception. Sometimes a person called the Presenter acted as showman to the play, and, probably, made a few impromptu remarks to explain the story.

Another device, of which several examples survive, was known as the Induction—a little introductory passage. In the *Spanish Tragedy*, the spirit of Revenge and the Ghost of Don Adrea come on and watch the play; during the intervals between the Acts they comment on the events which have just taken place. Sometimes the Induction consists of certain 'spectators' who discuss the play and its author, and tell each other who the various characters are as they make their appearance. Thus in *Every Man out of His Humour* Jonson introduces two spectators, Cordatus and Mitis, who first discuss the play and the meaning of 'humours,' and then make appropriate comments as the action progresses. At the end of Act II, Scene i, they converse thus:

MITIS. Methinks, Cordatus, he dwelt somewhat too long on this scene; it hung in the hand.

CORDATUS. I see not where he could have insisted less, and to have made the humours perspicuous enough.

MIT. True, as his subject lies; but he might have altered the shape of his argument, and explicated them better in single scenes.

COR. That had been single indeed. Why, be they not the same persons in this, as they would have been in those? and is it not an object of more state, to behold the scene full, and relieved with variety of speakers to the end, than to see a vast empty stage, and the actors come in, one by one, as if they were dropt down with a feather into the eye of the spectators?

MIT. Nay, you are better traded with these things than I, and therefore I'll subscribe to your judgement; marry, you shall give me leave to make objections.

COR. O, what else? It is the special intent of the author you should do so; for thereby others, that are present, may as well be satisfied, who haply would object the same you would do.

MIT. So, sir; but when appears Macilente again?

COR. Marry, he stays but till our silence give him leave; here he comes, and with him Signor Deliro, a merchant, at whose house he is come to sojourn; make your own observation now, only transfer your thoughts to the city, with the scene: where, suppose they speak.

The phrase "here he comes" or more commonly "see where he comes," is very often used to draw the attention of the audience to the entrance of a new character.

A somewhat similar convention is used in *The Taming of the Shrew*, where the play is given for the benefit of Sly the Tinker. Indeed, a "play within a play" is frequent. One has already been described in the *Spanish Tragedy*; two other famous examples in Shakespeare occur in *Hamlet* and *A Midsummer-Night's Dream*. In Peele's *Old Wives Tale*, the Old Woman begins to tell a story which is acted in the play. This device crops up from time to time in modern plays. In *Secrets*, for instance, the old mother goes to sleep and 'dreams' the events which are shown in the play itself. The same convention is often to be found in the cinema. When a character wishes to tell a long story, he is first shown surrounded by his audience, then the picture 'dissolves' into the events which he is narrating, and, at the end, dissolves back to the original speaker.

The Play Scene in *Hamlet* is preceded by a 'dumb show' in which the action of the play which is to follow is first shown in silent pantomime. Dumb show is really a survival from the pre-Shakespearean period, but it had its uses, especially to picture events which the characters are supposed to see by supernatural means. A good example is the Vision of Eight Kings which appeared to Macbeth (Act IV, Sc. i). In *Friar Bacon and Friar Bungay*, the Friar by his magic art shows Prince Edward what is happening to Lacy and Margaret.

The Elizabethans loved horrors. They thoroughly enjoyed the spectacle of an execution for high treason when the condemned man was first half-hanged, then cut down, disembowelled, and finally hacked into pieces as a warning to others. But as the supply of traitors was uncertain, the theatres catered for these gruesome tastes by giving realistic scenes of bloodshed. Some good passages may be taken from the tragedy of *Antonio's Revenge*, a play written by Marston about 1600.

In this scene, Antonio leads the boy Julio, the son of his father Andrugio's murderer, to the tomb; the ghost of Andrugio demands revenge.

ANTONIO. Stay, stay, deare father, fright mine eyes
    no more.
Reuenge as swift as lightning bursteth forth,
And cleares his heart. Come, prettie tender childe,
It is not thee I hate, not thee I kill—
Thy fathers blood that flowes within thy veines,
It is I loath; is that, Reuenge must sucke.
I loue thy soule: and were my heart lapt vp
In any flesh, but in *Piero's* bloode,
I would thus kisse it: but being his: thus, thus,
And thus Ile punch it. Abandon feares.
Whil'st thy wounds bleede, my browes shall gush
    out teares.
    IULIO. So you will loue me, doe euen what you will.
    ANT. Now barkes the Wolfe against the full
    cheekt Moone.
Now Lyons halfe-clamd entrals roare for food.
Now croakes the toad, & night-crowes screech aloud,
Fluttering 'bout casements of departing soules.
Now gapes the graues, and through their yawnes let
    loose
Imprison'd spirits to reuisit earth:

And now swarte night, to swell thy hower out,
Behold I spurt warme bloode in thy blacke eyes.
                    From vnder the stage a groane.
ANT. Howle not thou pury mould, groan not ye
    graues.
Be dumbe all breath. Here stands *Andrugio's* sonne,
Worthie his father. So: I feele no breath—
His iawes are falne, his dislodg'd soule is fled:
And now there's nothing, but *Piero*, left.
He is all *Piero*, father all. This blood,
This breast, this heart, *Piero* all:
Whome thus I mangle. Spright of *Iulyo*,
Forget this was thy trunke. I liue thy friend.
Maist thou be twined with the softst imbrace
Of cleare eternitie: but thy fathers blood,
I thus make incense of, to vengeance.
Ghost of my poysoned Syre, sucke this fume:
To sweete reuenge perfume thy circling ayre,
With smoake of bloode. I sprinkle round his goare,
And dewe thy hearse, with these fresh reeking drops.
Loe thus I heaue my blood-died handes to heauen:
Euen like insatiate hell, still crying; More.
My heart hath thirsting Dropsies after goare.
Sound peace, and rest, to Church, night ghosts, and
    graues.
Blood cries for bloode; and murder murder craues[1].

Towards the end of the play, a casual stage-direction notes: *The conspirators binde Piero, pluck out his tongue, and triumph ouer him.* What more could anyone want?

Ghosts appeared often, though the more reputable dramatists used them sparingly. Shakespeare's most famous example is the ghost of Hamlet's father who probably originated in

---

[1] This passage has been reproduced from the original quarto. The spelling and punctuation are unaltered.

an old play. His other ghosts—Caesar's, for instance, in *Julius Caesar*, or Banquo's in *Macbeth*—are very shadowy spirits which haunt their murderers but do nothing.

Chapman, however, was very fond of a ghost, and in his *Revenge of Bussy D'Ambois*, Bussy's ghost plays a considerable part.

Another restriction which greatly influenced dramatic writers was the fact that all female parts were taken by boys, and the players seem usually to have had only two or three 'girls' in the company at a time. Boys could be very good in female parts—as can be seen from a modern school performance at Christmas time—but the quality of their acting was variable, and, unfortunately, as soon as a boy became really good, his voice broke. This is one explanation of the way in which Shakespeare's heroines seem to go into sets chronologically.

Elizabethan playgoers were much intrigued by the common trick of making a girl dress up as a young man, especially as the 'girl' was a boy. About 1598–1600, the Chamberlain's Company evidently included a boy who was remarkably good at impersonating girls of the tomboy type; for him Shakespeare created the parts of Rosalind, Beatrice and Viola. A few years later another boy actor became expert at creating tragic parts such as Lady Macbeth or Cleopatra. Again, at the close of Shakespeare's career, the Company had a very girlish 'girl' who was Perdita and Miranda. Of course, Shakespeare's success in making such a character as Cleopatra did not depend on the boy actor, but as he was a working-dramatist, it would obviously have been a waste of time for him to have written a play which the females of the company were not capable of acting. To some extent therefore the members of the company helped the dramatist.

But parts were not only written for the chief members of the company. Sometimes a play-house had a particular attraction such as the Welsh singer who appeared as Lady Mortimer in the first part of *Henry the Fourth*; as Shake-speare knew no Welsh he added a stage direc-tion: *Here the Lady sings a Welsh song*; and left it to the actor. Special parts are, indeed, often quite easily traceable in the plays, and, by noting the physical peculiarities of a character, we can often form an estimate of the actor for whom Shakespeare intended the part. Thus Sir An-drew is "as tall as any man in Illyria" and Cassius has "a lean and hungry look."

Another dramatic convention which is not used nowadays by the greatest modern play-wrights (though it often occurs in melodrama) is known as the soliloquy. Soliloquies, as the name implies, are speeches delivered by the actor alone on the stage who thinks out aloud for the benefit of the audience. Such speeches are very common and vary in degree from the crude "I am the villain of the piece" to the wonderful self-revelations which Shakespeare gives in the dramas of his Tragic Period.

Shakespeare
The Tragic Period
1601–1607

W ITH the turn of the century, Shakespeare's outlook on life altered. The
sunshine of *As You Like It* disappears and is
succeeded by the storm and stress of *Hamlet*,
Macbeth and *Lear*. These years (1601–1607)
are often called Shakespeare's Tragic Period
because a feeling of pessimism, sometimes even
bitter despair, is predominant. This does not
necessarily mean that Shakespeare passed through
any personal suffering; for it was a time of
general gloom and the same pessimism can be
felt in the plays of other dramatists.

The change of outlook coincides with a new
method. It began when Shakespeare was writing
his mature Comedies. With the *First Part of
Henry the Fourth*, he may be said, for the first
time, to have completely mastered his material.
Henceforward he was a master-craftsman, free
to experiment or develop his dramatic ideas without having to trouble about the technical part
of the business.

In the early plays, Shakespeare treats all his
characters alike. We watch their adventures as
we should watch the adventures of pleasing and
very lively strangers. Then he begins to pick

out a character here and there for special treatment and he shows just a little more of that one person than of the others.

Perhaps the first great character to be treated in this way is Jaques, who could quite easily be left out of *As You Like It* without any alteration of the plot. Yet we feel that we know more of Jaques than of any of the others in the play; not only because he appears on the stage more often but because Shakespeare has carefully added more of those little touches which bring out Jaques' peculiar traits. The same thing happens in *Much Ado*; rather more care is devoted to Benedick and Beatrice than to the rest of the characters, yet the adventures of these two belong to the secondary plot.

From elaborating certain characters, Shakespeare comes gradually to show the play from the point of view of one man or group. We can illustrate this difference in his attitude by a simple common experience. When we watch a cricket match between two teams of strangers, we are interested in the game; but when we watch a team of our friends, we are less interested in the game than in their individual fortunes.

The Tragic Period opens with *Julius Caesar*, which is in the form of a Chronicle Play. But *Julius Caesar* is rightly classed with the tragedies; it is the tragedy of Brutus. The whole story is unfolded as it appeared to Brutus' eyes. Shakespeare produces this effect in a number of ways. For one thing, Brutus is shown as a high-minded idealist, whilst Caesar is intentionally portrayed at his very worst, as a rather feeble, superstitious tyrant. Several times Brutus reveals the workings of his mind so that we know exactly why he took the course he did; Caesar is never given any chance of explaining himself. And underneath the play, there is heard a new and more solemn note; the idea that

> There's a divinity that shapes our ends,
> Rough-hew them how we will.

Now at the maturity of his genius, Shakespeare returned to Tragedy. During the eight years in which he had been writing plays, his imagination had been growing as rapidly and powerfully as his technical skill. Henceforward, when a tragic story was laid before him, he not only saw it in his imagination, but he became part of it.

After *Julius Caesar* came *Hamlet*, the most fascinating if not the greatest of all Shakespeare's plays. The story was well known to Elizabethan playgoers; indeed, it is certain that so far as the plot is concerned, Shakespeare rewrote an old 'Revenge Play,' perhaps originally written by Kyd.

A comparison between the *Spanish Tragedy* and *Hamlet* will show what Shakespeare did for drama. Kyd's play tells simply of fierce, violent, elemental passions. These passions are still present in *Hamlet*, but they burn underground, and, in place of a Hieronimo, with his one thought of vengeance and his simple, almost animal, sorrow for his only son, Shakespeare creates a Hamlet who holds up the mirror to his age. Hamlet is the supreme portrait in literature of the Renaissance nobleman.

Hamlet's character is much misunderstood. Many critics suggest that he is one of those men who are too sensitive to survive in the brutal surroundings in which fate has placed them. But this is a false view. The Elizabethans lived in brutal, uncertain times and they knew nothing of our modern super-sensitiveness. At the same time they were not mere savages. Men of acute mind and boundless courage, like Sir Walter Raleigh, could go a-voyaging to the Indies with only the smallest hope of coming back, could puzzle over the secrets of the Universe, adore its beauty, enjoy its pleasures,

> And now and then stab, as occasion served.

Hamlet shows all these traits. He is Shakespeare's highest individual character; the example of his own words:

> What a piece of work is a man! how noble in reason! how infinite in faculty! in form and moving how express and admirable! In action how like an angel! in apprehension how like a god! the beauty of the world! the paragon of animals!

In the play, Shakespeare looks through Hamlet's eyes, almost identifies himself with Hamlet, and as a result, he is more concerned with what goes on in Hamlet's mind than in the outward details of the story. Again and again some little incident is introduced in order that Hamlet may display some corner of his many-sided nature.

The 'Grave-digging' Scene (Act v, Sc. i) will bring out Hamlet's nature as well as any.

The Grave-digger and his mate prepare to dig Ophelia's grave.

1ST CLOWN. Is she to be buried in Christian burial that wilfully seeks her own salvation?

2ND CLOWN. I tell thee she is: and therefore make her grave straight: the crowner hath sat on her, and finds it Christian burial.

1ST CLO. ⟨*who knows all about the law*⟩. How can that be, unless she drowned herself in her own defence?

2ND CLO. Why, 'tis found so.

1ST CLO. It must be 'se offendendo'; it cannot be else. For here lies the point: if I drown myself wittingly, it argues an act: and an act hath three branches; it is, to act, to do, to perform: argal, she drowned herself wittingly.

2ND CLO. Nay, but hear you, goodman delver,—

1ST CLO. ⟨*interrupting him*⟩. Give me leave. Here lies the water; good: here stands the man; good: if the man go to this water, and drown himself, it is, will he, nill he, he goes,—mark you that; but if the water come to him and drown him, he drowns not himself: argal, he that is not guilty of his own death shortens not his own life.

2ND CLO. But is this law?

1ST CLO. Ay, marry, is't; crowner's quest law.

2ND CLO. Will you ha' the truth on't? If this had not been a gentlewoman, she should have been buried out o' Christian burial.

1ST CLO. Why, there thou say'st: and the more pity that great folk should have countenance in this world to drown or hang themselves, more than their even Christian. Come, my spade. There is no ancient gentlemen but gardeners, ditchers, and grave-makers: they hold up Adam's profession.

2ND CLO. Was he a gentleman?

1st clo. He was the first that ever bore arms.

2nd clo. Why, he had none.

1st clo. What, art a heathen? How dost thou understand the Scripture? The Scripture says 'Adam digged': could he dig without arms? I'll put another question to thee: if thou answerest me not to the purpose, confess thyself—

2nd clo. Go to.

1st clo. What is he that builds stronger than either the mason, the shipwright, or the carpenter?

2nd clo. The gallows-maker; for that frame outlives a thousand tenants.

1st clo. I like thy wit well, in good faith: the gallows does well; but how does it well? it does well to those that do ill: now thou dost ill to say the gallows is built stronger than the church: argal, the gallows may do well to thee. To 't again, come.

2nd clo. 'Who builds stronger than a mason, a shipwright, or a carpenter?'

1st clo. Ay, tell me that, and unyoke.

2nd clo. Marry, now I can tell.

1st clo. To 't.

2nd clo. Mass, I cannot tell.

Hamlet, who has just returned to Denmark after his escape from the pirate ship, enters with Horatio at the back of the stage.

1st clo. Cudgel thy brains no more about it, for your dull ass will not mend his pace with beating; and, when you are asked this question next, say 'a grave-maker': the houses that he makes last till doomsday. Go, get thee to Yaughan: fetch me a stoup of liquor.   ⟨*Exit* 2nd clo.⟩

He takes off four waistcoats one after another[1], spits on his hands and begins to dig. As he digs, he sings:

[1] An old stage tradition.

In youth, when I did love, did love,
  Methought it was very sweet,
To contract, O, the time, for, ah, my behove,
  O, methought, there was nothing meet.

Hamlet and Horatio approach and look on.

HAMLET. Has this fellow no feeling of his business, that he sings at grave-making?

HORATIO. Custom hath made it in him a property of easiness.

HAM. 'Tis e'en so: the hand of little employment hath the daintier sense.

IST CLO. ⟨*Sings.*⟩
  But age, with his stealing steps,
    Hath claw'd me in his clutch,
  And hath shipped me intil the land,
    As if I had never been such.
              ⟨*Throws up a skull.*⟩

HAM. That skull had a tongue in it, and could sing once: how the knave jowls it to the ground, as if it were Cain's jaw-bone, that did the first murder! It might be the pate of a politician, which this ass now o'er-reaches; one that would circumvent God, might it not?

HOR. It might, my lord.

HAM. Or of a courtier; which could say 'Good morrow, sweet lord! How dost thou, good lord?' This might be my lord such-a-one, that praised my lord such-a-one's horse, when he meant to beg it; might it not?

HOR. Ay, my lord.

HAM. Why, e'en so: and now my Lady Worm's; chapless, and knocked about the mazzard with a sexton's spade: here's fine revolution, an we had the trick to see't. Did these bones cost no more the breeding, but to play at loggats with 'em? mine ache to think on't.

1ST CLO. ⟨*Sings.*⟩

    A pick-axe, and a spade, a spade,
      For and a shrouding sheet:
    O, a pit of clay for to be made
      For such a guest is meet.

              ⟨*Throws up another skull.*⟩

HAM. There's another: why may not that be the skull of a lawyer? Where be his quiddities now, his quillets, his cases, his tenures, and his tricks? why does he suffer this rude knave now to knock him about the sconce with a dirty shovel, and will not tell him of his action of battery? Hum! This fellow might be in's time a great buyer of land, with his statutes, his recognizances, his fines, his double vouchers, his recoveries: is this the fine of his fines, and the recovery of his recoveries, to have his fine pate full of fine dirt? will his vouchers vouch him no more of his purchases, and double ones too, than the length and breadth of a pair of indentures? The very conveyances of his lands will hardly lie in this box; and must the inheritor himself have no more, ha?

HOR. Not a jot more, my lord.

HAM. Is not parchment made of sheep-skins?

HOR. Ay, my lord, and of calf-skins too.

HAM. They are sheep and calves which seek out assurance in that. I will speak to this fellow. Whose grave's this, sirrah?

1ST CLO. Mine, sir.

⟨*Sings.*⟩   O, a pit of clay for to be made
          For such a guest is meet.

HAM. I think it be thine, indeed; for thou liest in't.

1ST CLO. You lie out on't, sir, and therefore it is not yours: for my part, I do not lie in't, and yet it is mine.

HAM. Thou dost lie in't, to be in't and say it is thine: 'tis for the dead, not for the quick; therefore thou liest.

1ST CLO. 'Tis a quick lie, sir; 'twill away again, from me to you.

HAM. What man dost thou dig it for?

1ST CLO. For no man, sir.

HAM. What woman, then?

1ST CLO. For none, neither.

HAM. Who is to be buried in't?

1ST CLO. One that was a woman, sir; but, rest her soul, she's dead.

HAM. How absolute the knave is! we must speak by the card, or equivocation will undo us. By the Lord, Horatio, these three years I have taken a note of it; the age is grown so picked that the toe of the peasant comes so near the heel of the courtier, he galls his kibe. How long hast thou been a grave-maker?

1ST CLO. Of all the days i' the year, I came to't that day that our last king Hamlet overcame Fortinbras.

HAM. How long is that since?

1ST CLO. Cannot you tell that? every fool can tell that: it was the very day that young Hamlet was born; he that is mad, and sent into England.

HAM. Ay, marry, why was he sent into England?

1ST CLO. Why, because he was mad: he shall recover his wits there; or, if he do not, it's no great matter there.

HAM. Why?

1ST CLO. 'Twill not be seen in him there; there the men are as mad as he.

HAM. How came he mad?

1ST CLO. Very strangely, they say.

HAM. How strangely?

1ST CLO. Faith, e'en with losing his wits.

HAM. Upon what ground?

1ST CLO. Why, here in Denmark: I have been sexton here, man and boy, thirty years.

HAM. How long will a man lie i' the earth ere he rot?

1ST CLO. I' faith, if he be not rotten before he die—as we have many pocky corses now-a-days, that will scarce hold the laying in—he will last you some eight year or nine year: a tanner will last you nine year.

HAM. Why he more than another?

1ST CLO. Why, sir, his hide is so tanned with his trade, that he will keep out water a great while; and your water is a sore decayer of your whoreson dead body. Here's a skull now; this skull has lain in the earth three and twenty years.

HAM. Whose was it?

1ST CLO. A whoreson mad fellow's it was: whose do you think it was?

HAM. Nay, I know not.

1ST CLO. A pestilence on him for a mad rogue! a' poured a flagon of Rhenish on my head once. This same skull, sir, was Yorick's skull, the king's jester.

HAM. This?

1ST CLO. E'en that.

HAM. Let me see. ⟨*Takes the skull.*⟩ Alas, poor Yorick! I knew him, Horatio: a fellow of infinite jest, of most excellent fancy: he hath borne me on his back a thousand times; and now, how abhorred in my imagination is it! my gorge rises at it. Here hung those lips that I have kissed I know not how oft. Where be your gibes now? your gambols? your songs? your flashes of merriment, that were wont to set the table on a roar? Not one now, to mock your own grinning? quite chap-fallen? Now get you to my lady's chamber, and tell her, let her paint an inch thick, to this favour she must come; make her laugh at that. Prithee, Horatio, tell me one thing.

HOR. What's that, my lord?

HAM. Dost thou think Alexander looked o' this fashion i' the earth?

HOR. E'en so.

HAM. And smelt so? pah!   ⟨*Puts down the skull.*⟩

HOR. E'en so, my lord.

HAM. To what base uses we may return, Horatio! Why may not imagination trace the noble dust of Alexander, till he find it stopping a bung-hole?

HOR. 'Twere to consider too curiously, to consider so.

HAM. No, faith, not a jot; but to follow him with modesty enough, and likelihood to lead it: as thus: Alexander died, Alexander was buried, Alexander returneth into dust; the dust is earth; of earth we make loam; and why of that loam, whereto he was converted, might they not stop a beer-barrel?

Imperious Caesar, dead and turn'd to clay,
Might stop a hole to keep the wind away:
O, that that earth, which kept the world in awe,
Should patch a wall to expel the winter's flaw!
But soft! but soft! aside: here comes the king.

At this point the funeral procession enters.

This episode between Hamlet and the Clown is to some extent a digression in the play, it serves to delay the story, otherwise it has little to do with the progress of the plot; but it does show how Shakespeare, at the height of his genius, was concerned with problems far deeper than the mere plot.

In all the great tragedies we feel that, behind and above the actual events, great Powers are moving. In *Julius Caesar*, Brutus and Cassius murder Caesar, but Caesar's spirit is too strong for them. *Macbeth*, too, is something more than a character study of an ambitious tyrant who does not shrink from murdering his king when a guest in his own house. Just as Aeschylus had considered the moral problems behind his stories, so Shakespeare, in his tragic period, considers not so much the story of an ambitious man as Ambition itself; not Hamlet, or Lear as "a man more sinned against than sinning," but Life itself.

We have seen how in so early a play as *The Merchant of Venice* Shakespeare could create the 'atmosphere' of a warm Italian night. In his Tragic Period he tried and succeeded with far harder themes. A very fine example of such 'atmosphere' is to be found in *Macbeth* in the scenes showing the murder of King Duncan.

Macbeth, who is already Thane of Glamis, has been hailed by the Weird Sisters as Thane of Cawdor and King hereafter. The first prophecy is fulfilled within a few moments of its utterance and this encourages Macbeth whose ambition has already stirred his thoughts to treason. He tells his wife, and she never leaves him until he promises to murder Duncan who is at the moment a guest under their roof.

Macbeth is an imaginative, moody man; he covets Duncan's throne but is sickened at the thought of the deed which is before him. As he goes in to Duncan's chamber, Lady Macbeth slips out at the other door and listens.

> LADY MACBETH. That which hath made them
>   drunk hath made me bold;
> What hath quench'd them hath given me fire. Hark!
>   Peace!
> It was the owl that shriek'd, the fatal bellman,
> Which gives the stern'st good night. He is about it:
> The doors are open; and the surfeited grooms
> Do mock their charge with snores: I have drugg'd
>   their possets,

That death and nature do contend about them,
Whether they live or die.

Macbeth's voice is heard from within.

MACBETH. Who's there? what, ho!

LADY M. Alack, I am afraid they have awaked,
And 'tis not done. The attempt and not the deed
Confounds us. Hark! I laid their daggers ready;
He could not miss 'em. Had he not resembled
My father as he slept, I had done't.

Macbeth comes back, his hands smeared with
blood. He moves listlessly, as if in a trance.

My husband!

MACB. I have done the deed. Didst thou not hear a
noise?

LADY M. I heard the owl scream and the crickets
cry.

Did not you speak?

MACB.　　　　When?

LADY M.　　　　　Now.

MACB.　　　　　　As I descended?

LADY M. Ay.

MACB. Hark!

Who lies i' the second chamber?

LADY M.　　　　Donalbain.

MACB. ⟨*Looking on his hands*⟩. This is a sorry sight.

LADY M. A foolish thought, to say a sorry sight.

MACB. ⟨*in an even dazed tone*⟩. There's one did
laugh in's sleep, and one cried 'Murder!'

That they did wake each other: I stood and heard
them:

But they did say their prayers, and address'd them
Again to sleep.

LADY M.　　There are two lodged together.

MACB. One cried 'God bless us!' and 'Amen' the
other;

As they had seen me with these hangman's hands.

Listening their fear, I could not say 'Amen,'
When they did say 'God bless us!'
 LADY M.   Consider it not so deeply.
 MACB. But wherefore could not I pronounce
  'Amen'?
I had most need of blessing, and 'Amen'
Stuck in my throat.
 LADY M.   These deeds must not be thought
After these ways; so, it will make us mad.
 MACB. ⟨*goes on with his tale, unconscious of his wife*⟩.
  Methought I heard a voice cry 'Sleep no more!
Macbeth does murder sleep,' the innocent sleep,
Sleep that knits up the ravell'd sleave of care,
The death of each day's life, sore labour's bath,
Balm of hurt minds, great nature's second course,
Chief nourisher in life's feast,—
 LADY M.   What do you mean?
 MACB. Still it cried 'Sleep no more!' to all the house:
'Glamis hath murder'd sleep, and therefore Cawdor
Shall sleep no more; Macbeth shall sleep no more.'
 LADY M. Who was it that thus cried? Why, worthy
  thane,
You do unbend your noble strength, to think
So brainsickly of things. ⟨*Guiding him to the door.*⟩
  Go get some water,
And wash this filthy witness from your hand.
Why did you bring these daggers from the place?
They must lie there: go carry them; and smear
The sleepy grooms with blood.
 MACB. ⟨*turning back*⟩. I'll go no more:
I am afraid to think what I have done;
Look on 't again I dare not.
 LADY M.   Infirm of purpose!
Give me the daggers: the sleeping and the dead
Are but as pictures: 'tis the eye of childhood
That fears a painted devil. If he do bleed,
I'll gild the faces of the grooms withal;
For it must seem their guilt. ⟨*Exit. Knocking within.*⟩

Lady Macbeth goes back to the death chamber. Suddenly there is a loud knocking on the outer door. Macbeth starts.

MACB.   Whence is that knocking?
How is't with me, when every noise appals me?
What hands are here? ha! they pluck out mine eyes.
Will all great Neptune's ocean wash this blood
Clean from my hand? No, this my hand will rather
The multitudinous seas incarnadine,
Making the green one red.

Lady Macbeth comes back; her hands, too, are smeared with blood.

LADY M. My hands are of your colour; but I shame
To wear a heart so white. ⟨*The knocking is heard again.*⟩ I hear a knocking
At the south entry: retire we to our chamber:
A little water clears us of this deed:
How easy is it, then! Your constancy
Hath left you unattended. ⟨*The knocking again.*⟩ Hark!
    more knocking.
Get on your nightgown, lest occasion call us,
And show us to be watchers. Be not lost
So poorly in your thoughts.
    MACB. To know my deed, 'twere best not know
    myself. ⟨*The knocking is repeated impatiently.*⟩
Wake Duncan with thy knocking! I would thou
    couldst!   ⟨*Macbeth follows his wife in.*⟩

The knocking continues. Then the Porter, rather the worse for sleep and drink, shuffles out, muttering.

PORTER. Here's a knocking indeed! If a man
were porter of hell-gate, he should have old turning
the key. ⟨*Knocking.*⟩ Knock, knock, knock! Who's
there, i' the name of Beelzebub? Here's a farmer,
that hanged himself on the expectation of plenty:

come in time; have napkins enow about you; here you'll sweat for't. ⟨*Knocking.*⟩ Knock, knock! Who's there, in the other devil's name? Faith, here's an equivocator, that could swear in both the scales against either scale; who committed treason enough for God's sake, yet could not equivocate to heaven: O, come in, equivocator. ⟨*Knocking.*⟩ Knock, knock, knock! Who's there? Faith, here's an English tailor come hither, for stealing out of a French hose: come in, tailor; here you may roast your goose. ⟨*Knocking.*⟩ Knock, knock; never at quiet! What are you? But this place is too cold for hell. I'll devil-porter it no further: I had thought to have let in some of all professions that go the primrose way to the everlasting bonfire. ⟨*Knocking.*⟩ Anon, anon! I pray you, remember the porter.   ⟨*Opens the gate.*⟩

⟨MACDUFF *and* LENNOX *enter.*⟩

MACD. Was it so late, friend, ere you went to bed, That you do lie so late?

PORT. 'Faith, sir, we were carousing till the second cock: and drink, sir, is a great provoker.

MACD. I believe drink gave thee the lie last night.

PORT. That it did, sir, i' the very throat on me: but I requited him for his lie; and, I think, being too strong for him, though he took up my legs sometime, yet I made a shift to cast him.

MACD. Is thy master stirring?

Macbeth, now quite composed, comes out to greet the new-comers.

Our knocking has awaked him; here he comes.

The appearance of the fuddled porter, pretending that he is the keeper of Hell Gate, and all unwittingly speaking the truth, is a wonderful example of 'comic relief.' The audience, as has been shown, demanded a Clown, and Shakespeare gave them their wish; but he chose his own time, with the result that this burst of drunken laughter in the silent house of death is one of the most terrible passages in tragic literature.

Many critics claim that *Lear* is Shakespeare's greatest play, so great that the emotions which a good actor can arouse are far too poignant for most audiences. After the Restoration, Nahum Tate altered the play and gave it a happy ending, and this version was acted by the great Garrick. Such liberties are not tolerated nowadays, with the result that until recently *Lear* was seldom seen on the stage.

The original story was not particularly tragic; Lear did not go mad under the strain of his sufferings and all turned out well in the end. But as Shakespeare developed the plot, the passions which he created were so terrible and awe-inspiring that no happy ending to Lear's sufferings could be found in this life.

King Lear was a proud old man with an uncontrollable temper; he was, too, a poor judge of character though, as it happened, his favourite daughter was also the only one who really loved him. At the beginning of the play, he feels that the time has come for him to divide the kingdom and spend the rest of his days with his youngest child. Unfortunately, at the very moment when he expects Cordelia to flatter his humour, she fails and humiliates him. Everything is thrown into confusion; he sends Cordelia packing and divides her share between his other two daughters, Regan and Goneril.

Lear's troubles now begin. Both daughters
resent his presence and treat him scornfully. In
his rage he dashes out into the night, accompanied only by his half-witted Fool. As the two
wander across the heath, a terrible storm breaks
over their heads and adds fuel to his passions.

LEAR. Blow, winds, and crack your cheeks! rage!
    blow!
You cataracts and hurricanoes, spout
Till you have drench'd our steeples, drown'd the cocks!
You sulphurous and thought-executing fires,
Vaunt-couriers to oak-cleaving thunderbolts,
Singe my white head! And thou, all-shaking thunder,
Smite flat the thick rotundity o' the world!
Crack nature's moulds, all germens spill at once,
That make ingrateful man!

FOOL. O nuncle, court holy-water in a dry house
is better than this rain-water out o' door. Good
nuncle, in, and ask thy daughters' blessing: here's
a night pities neither wise man nor fool.

LEAR. Rumble thy bellyful! Spit, fire! spout, rain!
Nor rain, wind, thunder, fire, are my daughters:
I tax not you, you elements, with unkindness;
I never gave you kingdom, call'd you children,
You owe me no subscription: then let fall
Your horrible pleasure; here I stand, your slave,
A poor, infirm, weak, and despised old man:
But yet I call you servile ministers,
That have with two pernicious daughters join'd
Your high engender'd battles 'gainst a head
So old and white as this. O! O! 'tis foul!

FOOL. He that has a house to put's head in has
a good head-piece.
            The man that makes his toe
                What he his heart should make
            Shall of a corn cry woe,
                And turn his sleep to wake.

For there was never yet fair woman but she made
mouths in a glass.

LEAR. No, I will be the pattern of all patience;
I will say nothing.

⟨*Enter* KENT.⟩

KENT. Who's there?

FOOL. Marry, here's grace and a cod-piece; that's
a wise man and a fool.

KENT. Alas, sir, are you here? things that love
   night
Love not such nights as these; the wrathful skies
Gallow the very wanderers of the dark,
And make them keep their caves: since I was man,
Such sheets of fire, such bursts of horrid thunder,
Such groans of roaring wind and rain, I never
Remember to have heard: man's nature cannot carry
The affliction nor the fear.

LEAR.   Let the great gods,
That keep this dreadful pother o'er our heads,
Find out their enemies now. Tremble, thou wretch,
That hast within thee undivulged crimes,
Unwhipp'd of justice: hide thee, thou bloody hand;
Thou perjured, and thou simular man of virtue
That art incestuous: caitiff, to pieces shake,
That under covert and convenient seeming
Hast practised on man's life: close pent-up guilts,
Rive your concealing continents, and cry
These dreadful summoners grace. I am a man
More sinn'd against than sinning.

KENT.   Alack, bare-headed!
Gracious my lord, hard by here is a hovel;
Some friendship will it lend you 'gainst the tempest:
Repose you there; while I to this hard house—
More harder than the stones whereof 'tis raised;
Which even but now, demanding after you,
Denied me to come in—return, and force
Their scanted courtesy.

LEAR. My wits begin to turn.
Come on, my boy: how dost, my boy? art cold?
I am cold myself. Where is this straw, my fellow?
The art of our necessities is strange,
That can make vile things precious. Come, your
    hovel.
Poor fool and knave, I have one part in my heart
That's sorry yet for thee.
    FOOL. ⟨*Singing.*⟩ He that has and a little tiny
      wit,—
With hey, ho, the wind and the rain,—
Must make content with his fortunes fit,
For the rain it raineth every day.
    LEAR. True, my good boy.
Come bring us to this hovel. ⟨*Exit Lear and Kent.*⟩

Thereafter Lear's passions swell beyond his control and he goes quite mad. At last he reaches his beloved Cordelia and with her finds rest. But war has now broken out. Lear and Cordelia are captured and in prison Cordelia, by Edmund's order, is murdered.

The messenger who had been sent to stop the murder has arrived too late. Lear enters carrying the body of Cordelia in his arms; his madness has once more come upon him. Edgar, Captain, and others following.

    LEAR. Howl, howl, howl, howl! O, you are men
      of stones:
Had I your tongues and eyes, I'ld use them so
That heaven's vault should crack. She's gone for
    ever!
I know when one is dead, and when one lives;
She's dead as earth. Lend me a looking-glass;
If that her breath will mist or stain the stone,
Why, then she lives.

KENT.   Is this the promised end?

EDGAR. Or image of that horror?

ALBANY.   Fall, and cease!

LEAR. This feather stirs: she lives! if it be so,
It is a chance which does redeem all sorrows
That ever I have felt.

KENT. ⟨*Kneeling.*⟩   O my good master!

LEAR. Prithee, away.

EDG.   'Tis noble Kent, your friend.

LEAR. A plague upon you, murderers, traitors all!
I might have saved her; now she's gone for ever!
Cordelia, Cordelia! stay a little. Ha!
What is't thou say'st? Her voice was ever soft,
Gentle, and low, an excellent thing in woman.
I kill'd the slave that was a-hanging thee.

CAPTAIN. 'Tis true, my lords, he did.

LEAR.   Did I not, fellow?
I have seen the day, with my good biting falchion
I would have made them skip: I am old now,
And these same crosses spoil me. Who are you?
Mine eyes are not o' the best: I'll tell you straight.

KENT. If fortune brag of two she loved and hated,
One of them we behold.

LEAR. This is a dull sight. Are you not Kent?

KENT.   The same,
Your servant Kent. Where is your servant Caius?

LEAR. He's a good fellow, I can tell you that;
He'll strike, and quickly too: he's dead and rotten.

KENT. No, my good lord; I am the very man,—

LEAR. I'll see that straight.

KENT. That, from your first of difference and
    decay,
Have follow'd your sad steps.

LEAR.   You are welcome hither.

KENT. Nor no man else: all's cheerless, dark, and
    deadly.
Your eldest daughters have fordone themselves,
And desperately are dead.

LEAR.   Ay, so I think.

ALB. He knows not what he says: and vain it is
That we present us to him.

EDG.   Very bootless.

⟨*Enter a* Captain.⟩

CAPT. Edmund is dead, my lord.

ALB.   That's but a trifle here.
You lords and noble friends, know our intent.
What comfort to this great decay may come
Shall be applied; for us, we will resign,
During the life of this old majesty,
To him our absolute power: ⟨*To Edgar and Kent*⟩
    you, to your rights;
With boot, and such addition as your honours
Have more than merited. All friends shall taste
The wages of their virtue, and all foes
The cup of their deservings. O, see, see!

LEAR. And my poor fool is hang'd! No, no, no life!
Why should a dog, a horse, a rat, have life,
And thou no breath at all? Thou'lt come no more,
Never, never, never, never, never!
Pray you, undo this button: thank you, sir.
Do you see this? Look on her, look, her lips,
Look there, look there!   ⟨*Dies.*⟩

EDG.   He faints! My lord, my lord!

KENT. Break, heart; I prithee, break!

EDG.   Look up, my lord.

KENT. Vex not his ghost: O, let him pass! he
    hates him much
That would upon the rack of this tough world
Stretch him out longer.

EDG.   He is gone, indeed.

KENT. The wonder is, he hath endured so long:
He but usurp'd his life.

ALB. Bear them from hence. Our present business
Is general woe. ⟨*To Kent and Edgar.*⟩ Friends of
    my soul, you twain

Rule in this realm, and the gored state sustain.

    KENT. I have a journey, sir, shortly to go;
My master calls me, I must not say no.

    ALB. The weight of this sad time we must obey;
Speak what we feel, not what we ought to say.
The oldest hath borne most: we that are young
Shall never see so much, nor live so long.

⟨Exeunt, with a dead march.⟩

No other ending is possible.

Conclusion

THE fact that historians usually begin a fresh chapter with the accession of a new king or dynasty has fostered the sub-conscious idea that the end of a reign marks clearly definable changes in everyday life. It is almost a fixed belief in school histories that whilst the age of Elizabeth was wholly glorious epoch, the age of James the First and his son was wholly regrettable. Hence comes the idea that 'Elizabethan' drama was solely the product of the 'Elizabethan' age.

In this matter fame has been unkind to James who was always a far more enthusiastic and enlightened patron of the drama than ever Queen Elizabeth had been. With the exception of *Hamlet*, all Shakespeare's great tragedies were written after 1603; *Othello* and *Lear* were performed at Court, and several passages in *Macbeth* were almost certainly written to flatter the king. It would therefore be fair to make a distinction between 'Elizabethan' and 'Jacobean' drama. Historically the Elizabethan age really came to an end with the execution of the Earl of Essex on 25th February 1601. Thereafter the old Queen was too broken-hearted and too ill to take much interest in what went on around her.

Elizabethan drama can be grouped for convenience into three divisions. The first begins in 1586 with Kyd's *Spanish Tragedy*, followed by all the plays of Marlowe and Greene, and the very earliest of Shakespeare's works.

Dramatists are as yet mainly concerned with vivid action and fine speeches. For the most part there is little subtlety about the motives or sufferings of heroes and villains, the whole outlook being that of children who say "Tell us a story."

This first period, too, saw the great vogue of the Chronicle Play. In August 1588, the Spanish Armada had been defeated and, perhaps for the first time, Englishmen had become fully conscious of their nationality. Since the beginning of the reign, the idea that England was a great European power had been growing. As time went on, partly as the result of religious intolerance on both sides, partly because of the rough-and-ready methods of English seamen, Englishmen had ceased to be regarded by other European nations as quaint creatures from the barbarous North, but as men who were to be treated with considerable respect. There were other causes, too numerous to be mentioned here, that contributed to the growth of the national spirit which had so great an influence on English drama. It shows itself in the Chronicle Plays. Men suddenly realised that England had a history as well as other countries and that such heroes as Henry the Fifth could make almost as good a show as Tamburlaine.

Good Chronicle Plays are exceedingly difficult

to write, but even poor ones are fairly certain of being acceptable to an audience which loves to see 'real' events acted before them. It is a natural instinct; there are few who have not secretly regretted that they were not present at the battle of Agincourt or the Siege of Troy; and the stage gave the best possible substitute for the real thing. But History Plays are not usually high art; they have none of the interest of a tragedy of human events which might happen to any one of us.

The first great dramatists hardly realised the possibilities of their art. They produced striking situations; plots with plenty of action and many long speeches, some with magnificent ringing periods, some merely windy and bombastic. But they seldom, if ever, attempted to portray complicated motives or the sufferings of the soul. Had Marlowe lived, he might perhaps have produced such a play. Indeed in *Faustus*, he does consider the psychology of the great peasant scholar of Wittenberg, and that last soliloquy as Faustus sees his doom approach minute by minute, is one of the finest pictures of mental anguish in all literature. But Marlowe died young and in *Edward the Second* he had already dropped the psychological method. The first period ends with his death in 1593.

The second period runs from 1594 to 1601— not, of course, that 'periods' end distinctly like railway lines; their beginnings and endings are as vague as the edges of a mist. During these years Shakespeare produced his early apprentice plays and very rapidly—in no more than three years—progressed from the immaturities of *A Midsummer-Night's Dream* to the perfect balance of *Henry the Fourth*. This was the flowering time of the Elizabethan age. The victory over the Armada was the most economical in history; and so cheaply was it bought that England suffered few of the inconveniences of peace with which we are now so familiar. Feelings of triumph and satisfaction were enhanced by increasing prosperity.

In drama the general tone in the most memorable plays is one of satisfaction; "God's in his heaven, all's well with the world." And then gradually a change comes; the sunshine disappears. Events became less stirring and a period of reflection succeeded the years of action. Moreover, certain definite changes threatened. Queen Elizabeth was growing old; the courtiers and councillors who had been brought up with her were disappearing and the new generation, which had seen little of her greatness, found little to admire in her declining years. Factions and bitterness increased in the Court which was now dominated by the Earl of Essex but ruled by Sir Robert Cecil and his clique of politicians. The climax was reached when Essex went to Ireland, failed, rebelled and died as a traitor. Shakespeare's England was a small place and history was chiefly made in London. Naturally then the tone of the London theatres, always quick to react to popular feelings, changed from content to pessimism.

This air of pessimism increased in the third period to which the dates 1601 to 1607 may roughly be assigned. It corresponds in some ways to these present post-war times when writers and thinkers are, almost without exception, full of woeful prognostications of the immediate end of civilisation. Pessimism took rather a different course in those days; the reaction did not go so far; and the general attitude of thoughtful men was one of inquiry into a life which seemed sometimes senselessly cruel, sometimes simply futile. In drama, this spirit shows itself in the satirical comedies of Jonson and the great tragedies of Shakespeare, where

this goodly frame, the earth, seems to me a sterile promontory, this excellent canopy, the air, look you, this brave o'er-hanging firmament, this majestical roof fretted with golden fire, why it appears no other thing to me than a foul and pestilent congregation of vapours.

It was a time of problem plays. Dramatists, such as Marston, delighting in the horrible and the terrible, worked out on the stage stories of revolting sins and abnormal crimes. Even Shakespeare was affected by these problems, as is shown by such plays as *Measure for Measure*, *Othello* and *Timon*.

With 1607 the story of Elizabethan drama may be brought to a close. The great writers of the next generation—Jonson, Ford, Massinger, Webster, Beaumont and Fletcher—wrote for different audiences and in the changed conditions of London under the first of the Stuarts.

Shakespeare had now almost finished. He had retired for most of his time to his home in Stratford; but at the end of his career (1610–12) he produced *The Winter's Tale* and *The Tempest*, which are really the last roses of the Elizabethan age. There is a note of mature tranquillity and reconciliation with life in these plays which does not appear elsewhere. For the old generation

> Sleepe after toyle, port after stormie seas,
> Ease after warre, death after life does greatly please.

The reward of advancing years is to be found in the happiness of the new generation.

If these plays reflect Shakespeare's own feelings, perhaps they are the result of the quiet of the country after the intrigues of the city. *The Winter's Tale*, indeed, smells of the country when Perdita distributes flowers at the sheep-shearing feast:

> Here's flowers for you;
> Hot lavender, mints, savory, marjoram;
> The marigold, that goes to bed wi' the sun
> And with him rises weeping: these are flowers
> Of middle summer, and I think they are given
> To men of middle age. You're very welcome.
> CAMILLO. I should leave grazing, were I of your flock,
> And only live by gazing.
> PERDITA. Out, alas!
> You'ld be so lean, that blasts of January
> Would blow you through and through. Now, my fair'st friend,
> I would I had some flowers o' the spring that might

Become your time of day; and yours, and yours,
That wear upon your virgin branches yet
Your maidenheads growing: O Proserpina,
For the flowers now, that frighted thou let'st fall
From Dis's waggon! daffodils,
That come before the swallow dares, and take
The winds of March with beauty; violets dim,
But sweeter than the lids of Juno's eyes
Or Cytherea's breath; pale primroses,
That die unmarried, ere they can behold
Bright Phœbus in his strength—a malady
Most incident to maids; bold oxlips and
The crown imperial; lilies of all kinds,
The flower-de-luce being one! O, these I lack,
To make you garlands of, and my sweet friend,
To strew him o'er and o'er!

Shakespeare ended his work with a play of
reconciliation—*The Tempest*. It is a wonderful
story of a magic island wherein Prospero,
magician and sometime Duke of Milan, has
been stranded with his daughter Miranda.
Hither by his art, Prospero brings his ancient
enemies and in the end ancient wrongs are
righted in the new generation—Ferdinand and
Miranda.

The moment for Prospero's triumph has
arrived. He enters, clad in his magic robes,
with his attendant spirit Ariel.

PROSPERO. Now does my project gather to a head:
My charms crack not; my spirits obey; and time
Goes upright with his carriage. How's the day?
ARIEL. On the sixth hour; at which time, my lord,
You said our work should cease.
PROS.   I did say so,
When first I raised the tempest. Say, my spirit,
How fares the king and's followers?

ARI.   Confined together
In the same fashion as you gave in charge,
Just as you left them; all prisoners, sir,
In the line-grove which weather-fends your cell;
They cannot budge till your release. The king,
His brother and yours, abide all three distracted
And the remainder mourning over them,
Brimful of sorrow and dismay; but chiefly
Him that you term'd, sir, 'The good old lord, Gon-
      zalo';
His tears run down his beard, like winter's drops
From eaves of reeds. Your charm so strongly works
      'em
That if you now beheld them, your affections
Would become tender.
PROS.   Dost thou think so, spirit?
ARI. Mine would, sir, were I human.
PROS.   And mine shall.
Hast thou, which art but air, a touch, a feeling
Of their afflictions, and shall not myself,
One of their kind, that relish all as sharply,
Passion as they, be kindlier moved than thou art?
Though with their high wrongs I am struck to the
      quick,
Yet with my nobler reason 'gainst my fury
Do I take part: the rarer action is
In virtue than in vengeance: they being penitent,
The sole drift of my purpose doth extend
Not a frown further. Go release them, Ariel:
My charms I'll break, their senses I'll restore,
And they shall be themselves.
ARI.   I'll fetch them, sir. ⟨*Exit.*⟩
PROS. Ye elves of hills, brooks, standing lakes and
      groves,
And ye that on the sands with printless foot
Do chase the ebbing Neptune and do fly him
When he comes back; you demi-puppets that
By moonshine do the green sour ringlets make,

Whereof the ewe not bites, and you whose pastime
Is to make midnight mushrooms, that rejoice
To hear the solemn curfew; by whose aid,
Weak masters though ye be, I have bedimm'd
The noontide sun, call'd forth the mutinous winds,
And 'twixt the green sea and the azured vault
Set roaring war: to the dread rattling thunder
Have I given fire and rifted Jove's stout oak
With his own bolt; the strong-based promontory
Have I made shake and by the spurs pluck'd up
The pine and cedar: graves at my command
Have waked their sleepers, oped, and let 'em forth
By my so potent art. But this rough magic
I here abjure, and, when I have required
Some heavenly music, which even now I do,
To work mine end upon their senses that
This airy charm is for, I'll break my staff,
Bury it certain fathoms in the earth,
And deeper than did ever plummet sound
I'll drown my book.   ⟨*Solemn music.*⟩

Thereafter Shakespeare, like Prospero, broke his staff and wrote no more.

Englishmen unanimously accept Shakespeare as the greatest of all English poets. "He was not of an Age but for all Time," because to no other man has been given such wisdom, humanity, and sympathy, or such mastery of human speech to express them.

But great men seldom come singly, and, as a dramatist, Shakespeare can be best appreciated in the company of the Elizabethan dramatists.

Bibliography

Most of the plays mentioned in this book are reprinted in *Everyman's Library* (Dent), which includes *The Plays of Christopher Marlowe* (383), *The Plays of Ben Jonson* (489, 490), *Minor Elizabethan Drama*; 1. *Pre-Shakesperian Tragedy* (contains *The Spanish Tragedy*); 2. *Pre-Shakesperian Comedy* (*Roister Doister, Endimion, Old Wives Tale, Friar Bacon* and *James the Fourth*) (491, 492).

There are innumerable editions of Shakespeare. The *Warwick Shakespeare* (Blackie) is perhaps the best for any one beginning the study of Shakespeare. The *Arden Shakespeare* (Methuen) is a useful library edition. The Cambridge University Press is at the present time bringing out *The New Shakespeare* (edited by Sir A. T. Quiller-Couch and Professor J. Dover Wilson) based on the most recent bibliographical discoveries. A *New Readers' Shakespeare*, edited on new lines, will shortly be published by Messrs Harrap & Co.

CRITICISM

W. HAZLITT. *The Characters of Shakespeare's Plays.* (Everyman's Library.)

ELIZABETH LEE. *A School History of English Literature.* (3 vols., Blackie.)

A. C. BRADLEY. *Shakesperean Tragedy.* (Macmillan.)

Sir A. T. QUILLER-COUCH. *Shakespeare's Workmanship.* (T. Fisher Unwin.)

Sir A. W. WARD. *A History of English Dramatic Literature to the Death of Queen Anne.* (3 vols., Macmillan.)

F. S. BOAS. *Shakespeare and his Predecessors.* (Murray.)

C. F. TUCKER BROOKE. *Tudor Drama.* (Constable.)

J. SPENS. *Elizabethan Drama.* (Methuen.)

BIOGRAPHY, ETC.

E. K. CHAMBERS. *The Elizabethan Stage.* (4 vols., Oxford.) The standard work on all matters connected with the Elizabethan stage.

Shakespeare's England. (2 vols., Oxford.) A very complete survey of Elizabethan England, each chapter being written by an expert.

Sir SIDNEY LEE. *A Life of William Shakespeare.* (Murray.) A most useful and complete book of reference for all matters connected with the life of Shakespeare.

Sir WALTER RALEIGH. *Shakespeare.* (English Men of Letters, Macmillan.) The best and most readable short critical account of the poet.

GREGORY SMITH. *Ben Jonson.* (English Men of Letters.) A good account of Jonson's methods, theories and work.

E. A. G. LAMBORN and G. B. HARRISON. *Shakespeare: The Man and His Stage.* (The World's Manuals, Oxford.) An account, with many illustrations, of the life of Shakespeare, his stage, times and texts.

G. B. HARRISON. *Shakespeare's Fellows.* (Lane.) An account of the lives and environment of the chief Elizabethan dramatists, including Kyd, Marlowe, Greene and Jonson.

J. DOVER WILSON. *Life in Shakespeare's England.* (Cambridge.) Extracts from contemporary literature illustrating various aspects of life in Elizabethan England.

Chronological Table

Note. IT IS OFTEN IMPOSSIBLE TO DATE A PLAY WITH
ANY GREAT ACCURACY; THIS LIST, IN MOST INSTANCES,
ONLY GIVES THE APPROXIMATE DATE

1553 (about) *Ralph Roister Doister.*
1554 (about) Lyly born.
1558 (about) Thomas Kyd born.
              Robert Greene born.
1560 *Gorboduc* produced.
1564 February. Christopher Marlowe born.
     April. William Shakespeare born.
1572 Ben Jonson born.
1576 The first English Theatre built.
1579 *Euphues* published.
1580 *Apologie for Poetrie* written.
1586 Death of Sir Philip Sidney.
     Spanish Tragedy.
1587 February. Mary Queen of Scots executed.
     Tamburlaine part I.
1588 *Tamburlaine* part II.
     August. Defeat of the Spanish Armada.
1589 *Dr Faustus.*
1590 *The Jew of Malta.*
1591 The last fight of the "Revenge."
     Endimion published.
     Edward the Second.
     Friar Bacon and Friar Bungay.
1592 *Henry the Sixth*, three parts.
     September. Robert Greene died.
     December. *The Groatsworth of Wit* published.
1593 May. Christopher Marlowe killed at Deptford.
1594 *Love's Labour's Lost.*
     Romeo and Juliet.

1595 *A Midsummer-Night's Dream.*
Richard the Second.
The Old Wives Tale.

1596 *The Merchant of Venice.*

1597 *Henry the Fourth,* part I.

1598 *Henry the Fourth,* part II.
August. Death of Lord Burleigh.
September. *Every Man in his Humour* produced.

1599 January to July. Building of the Globe Theatre.
Henry the Fifth.
Twelfth Night.
Much Ado about Nothing.
As You Like It.
Every Man out of his Humour.

1600 *Julius Caesar.*
Antonio's Revenge.

1601 Rebellion and execution of the Earl of Essex.
Hamlet (first version).
Satiromastix.

1603 March. Death of Queen Elizabeth. Accession
of King James the First.
May. The Chamberlain's men become the
King's Players.

1604 November. *Othello* acted at Court.

1605 November. Gunpowder Plot discovered.
Macbeth.

1606 December. *King Lear* acted at Court.

1611 *The Tempest.*

1616 April. William Shakespeare died.